I0437935

The Unbroken Chains of Apartheid

The Unbroken Chains of Apartheid

SOUTH AFRICA

Matsime Simon Mohapi

Copyright © 2011 by Matsime Simon Mohapi.

ISBN: Softcover   978-1-4628-8905-1
               Ebook   978-1-4628-8906-8

All rights reserved. No part of this book may be reproduced or transmitted in any
form or by any means, electronic or mechanical, including photocopying, recording,
or by any information storage and retrieval system, without permission in writing
from the copyright owner.

This book was printed in the United States of America.

To order additional copies of this book, contact:
Xlibris Corporation
0-800-891-366
www.xlibris.co.nz
Orders@ Xlibris.co.nz
302257

This book is dedicated to the ten hundred thousands of South Africans who continue to suffer the consequences of colonisation and apartheid in the new South Africa. It is also dedicated to the millions of the people in the world who continue to suffer the oppression of one by the other.

CONTENTS

AUTHOR'S NOTE

This book is an attempt to capture the lives of Black people in South Africa before the arrival of White people in 1652, before the Black people's residential security of possession and their livelihood and the destiny of us their children were put in trouble.

This book is an attempt to capture the lives of our ancestors; our forefathers and foremothers before they were forced at a gun barrel and canon to become foreigners in their motherland and before foreigners became at home in a foreign land—South Africa.

This book is an attempt to capture the lives of Black South Africans long before they were declared illegal denizens in the "White man's land"; long before they were given a forced "independent" dependency in barren homelands and Bantustans—in the most arid parts of South Africa.

This book is an attempt to capture the lives of Black people before it became a single note of sadness. To capture our lives before my great grandfather's great grandfather cried out: "Had I but died a day before 07 April 1652, I had lived a blessed time; for, from that day, there is nothing of contentment to the Black man; all is but agony. My pride is attacked. My single state of manhood is shaken. My humanity is killed and I am reduced to a mere less than human. And I am pushed to live and die in poverty."

This book is written so that my children, my grand children, my great grand children, and so on, should know where they come from. It is written so that your children, your grand children, and you great grand children, and so on, should know where they come from. It is written so that our children, our grand children, our great grand children, and so on, should know where they come from.

This book is written in the firm believe that children have the inherent right to know their past so that they may begin to understand how and why the find themselves where they are today. By understanding where they are and where they stand shall be a torch for them to illuminate their way forward to their destiny. Hundred times my grand father told me that he tells me of my past only because a real people is the one who knows himself by knowing his past which shall give him a sense of direction in life.

This book is written for both Black and White children who are in the ignorance of the land question and its wealth in South Africa. It is written for the Black and White children who do not know the politics of "*the land bought the land never sold*". It is written so that the Black and White children should not be caught unaware by the predictable cry and movement for equitable distribution of land and its wealth. It is written in the knowledge that children are innocent and always ready to share and thus they can positively encourage their parents to do the right thing in search of true change and true peace and true reconciliation in our beloved South Africa.

This book is written for both Black and White South Africans who want us to go back to the old South Africa of apartheid because they claim life was better there than here in the new South Africa. This book is written for people who are ignorant of our history before 1948 and apartheid. This book is written for the Black man who daily sinks deeper and deeper into the depths of poverty and blames the present government and praises the apartheid government. It is hoped that after reading this book, both Black and White people, shall have respect for the present government and its leaders.

This book shall deal with the agony suffered by the Blacks after the arrival of White people in South Africa. It shall deal with the agony and losses suffered during colonisation, the agony of being declared a foreigner in your motherland, the agony of being exterminated and destroyed mercilessly by the all powerful illegitimate governments solely to grab from you what rightly belongs to you and worst, the agony of being declared not a human being by apartheid government.

This book is aimed at digging out the truth so that the Whites could appreciate that the Blacks are a people of great suffering yet great forgivers and great role players for reconciliation in the new South Africa. Blacks are people who have so much to forgive, but who, in their generosity, do forgive. They are people who were taught at an early age that forgiveness is greater than revenge.

This book is aimed at awakening all South Africans to the truth that unless true change and equal sharing and equitable distribution of land and its wealth pact are reached, all is but agony for the Black people. And all is but toys.

By reading this book you allow me to hold your hand and walk with you the difficult terrain of blood, death and destruction of Black people's lives in South Africa from 1500 to 2011. When your hearts become too heavy and your knees too weak because of this painful living history, I shall patiently wait for you and pray that God comforts you. I know that you are not stones but people, so at the end of reading this book I hope that you, both Black and White South Africans, will stand up and play your part in bringing true change and true peace and true reconciliation to South Africa in our lifetime.

This book is written with the hope that after reading it all Black and White Political Parties in South Africa shall come together and form MTT: Movement for True Change and True Reconciliation. This is a humble call to all politicians to stand up and willingly meet each other half way towards true change and true reconciliation in our lifetime. The life and death of Black and White South Africans are in your hands. The death of poverty and the life of prosperity in South Africa are in your hands. It is up to you. As you think about the painful truth in this book you should not stop to pray: "God save South Africa. Guide her politicians. Guard her Black and White children. In our hearts plant the seeds of your love for one another. And give peace and prosperity to all in our lifetime. And Glory be to God. Amen."

Matsime Simon Mohapi, 02 May 2011

THE LIFE IN SOUTH AFRICA BEFORE 1652

Today the year is of the Lord 1500 and in other parts of the world people are celebrating Christmas. There are no Christmas celebrations in South Africa because the disciples of Jesus Christ have not yet arrived on this part of Africa and that is why Christianity is not known or practiced in South Africa today.

This morning a smiling great grandmother walking without the help of stick emerges from one of the homesteads and summons her thirty or so great grand children towards the center of the circle of her homesteads. She says to them: "*Bana ba nkgono, a Modimo o rorisoe; mathang le motse o na kaofela le bajweetse hore mona ha ntate Mohapi oa Thulo M'phete ho tsoetswe ngoana oa ngoanana. Bitso la hae e tla ba Pulane-Puleng ka hobane ho letse ho tsholoha ea maebana mabane bosiu ha a horoha*". Simply she says: "My great grandchildren let God be praised. Run all over all homesteads in the whole village in all directions and inform people that a baby girl is born to us. Her name shall be "Pulane" because she brought us rain." This is how the birth of a new born child was declared and made known to all the people in the African villages in all ages. They were given African names with meaning to Africa and its people.

This is the fact that ages before the birth of Jesus of Nazareth, Black people knew that there is the Creator of heaven and earth. In Setswana language they called the Creator of heaven and earth "Modimo", God in English. Africans were straightforward spiritual people of God.

They believed that God is present, reachable, active, providing, caring, and abides in heaven where He is reachable only through their ancestors. They maintained strong connections with their ancestors by performing cultural rituals like slaughtering a sheep or goat to thank them for whatever goodness they may have received in their lives from God the Creator in the Most Highness. Just like in the Holy Bible and before it was even written, the Black people used sacrifices as a means of communication—the actual slaughtering of a domestic animal, the pouring out of the blood, was believed to create a connection between man and God via the man's ancestors. They thanked their ancestors because they believed that their ancestors were making good intercession and representing them well before God the Creator. That is why even today, although somehow confused and turned back against African religion, some Africans; learned and unlearned, still perform "*Mpho ya Badimo or Go fa Badimo or Go kopa Badimo, jalojalo*".

They believed that God is God of the living and the dead. So those who are still alive and those who have died doing good belong to God. These ancestors were not worshipped, but were called on to help with this life's problems and to intercede for the living before God. Our ancestors were believed to be the living dead.

Characteristically they defined God as a God of goodness, truth, and beauty. Daily in their lives they strived to be good, truthful and the fact that they responded to beauty tells us that their spirits strived upwards to its source—God the Creator. Africans believed that being godly is living good and being good to others, being truthful to self and others, and that the beauty of God is found in the high spirits of each and every contented man, woman and child in the whole village. The African Kings were believed to represent the will of God on earth and were highly regarded. Their heavenly mandate was thought to be nothing but to ensure that there was goodness, truth and satisfaction to the people in the whole villages. Truth, goodness, and contentment resulted in law and order, stability and peace, and love and satisfaction in all villages. The fact is that there are still Black people in Africa today or they could have killed each other to extinction millenniums ago if there was no order, peace, and stability as we were wrongly taught in apartheid schools.

At school we were taught that Whites found the Blacks without God. They taught us like God landed at the Cape of Good Hope the same day with

Jan van Riebeeck. From the beginning Whites were not good to Blacks and it resulted in Blacks rejecting Whites and regrettably, rejecting "White Jesus the son of God". This "God the father of White Jesus Christ" shook and weakened the faith and believes of Black people in God. King Moshoeshoe of Basotho, refusing baptismal and conversion into Christianity, said: "If this God is the God of White Jesus Christ, White people, suffering, injustice, and oppression; then I would rather choose to live without him." The White people had succeeded to confuse and weaken believes and faith of Black people in God. The Whites knew that a people without God are weak and dead living. The Black people's experience of God, their understanding of who God is, what He is like and his involvement in their lives and human history, was destroyed by the coming of the Whites. Their faith in God was not fulfilled, but to most Blacks it was weakened and to some destroyed.

Surely King Moshoeshoe remained with many questions like: is the memory of the dead heathen? Is the memory and good influence the dead inculcated in us heathen? Is it wrong to remember and respect those who took care of us, loved us and provided for us? Is Jesus Christ the only ancestor? They could have at least said that Jesus is the "Principal Ancestor" who was sent by God to represent God on earth and he went back to the community of heaven to intercede and meditates between us and God the Creator. I think it could have made much sense to the people who respected ancestors and ancestry as Africans.

The fact that King Moshoeshoe never converted to Christianity is testified by his grave up there at Thaba Bosiho Mountain because it has no trace of a cross as a symbol of Christianity. I was there today and I realised that many centuries old graves have no crosses and not a single trace of a cross. What was most interesting to me up the mountain was to find that some graves are not in rectangular shape as of today but are in a circle shape because the dead were not lied down to rest but it was believed that they were going somewhere and a man cannot walk lying down on his back. So the grave of King Moshoeshoe's father is in the shape of a circle and it is written in Sesotho: "*Mona ke kemiso ea ha Ntate Mokhechane Moshoeshoe*".

But NO, South Africans, God was not brought to South Africa by Jan van Rieebeck and was not introduced to South Africans by the White people. The White people introduced Jesus Christ and the Bible and the Church at the highest cost and much injury to the Blacks; injury to their souls, spirits and livelihood. Black people had no holy Bible. They had no holy Church buildings for Sundays; but their daily lives were holy. They had an inborn sense of the Divine and innermost desire to reach out beyond them in order to discover God the Creator and find meaning for their lives. Their daily lives were one with God's will as they understood what God's will meant to them and in harmony to God's whole creation.

Black people believed that God is not a God of Sunday but a God of everyday. They believed that God is not found in buildings but in high spirits of each and every contented man, woman and child. Their thinking of God, their words and actions could not be separated in sayings only but in demonstrating and living what they believed in. They believed that God encompassed each facet of their being—birth, life, death, life after death, social relationships, culture, customs, Kings and Chiefs, people and subjects, law and morality, rain and seasons, crops, land, fields, animals and cattle.

God and their whole life went together. That is why our grandmothers sung praise songs to the Creator as they reap sweet soft maize and sugar cane from their own fields without waiting for Sunday to give praises. Their hearts were filled with gratitude and they were thankful everyday. They were thankful to God because they knew that it was God the Creator who gave them abundant life; that was, life of peace, happiness, and satisfaction.

Our ancestors sung hymns in praise to God the Creator when a child was born; they sung when the child graduated from our traditional school; they sung when the child got married; they sung when the child brought glory to their clan name; they sung when the dry season came; they sung when the rain season came; they sung when they worked the fields; they sung when they milked in oversupply; they sung when livestock multiplied in manifolds; they sung when they planted crops; they sung when they reaped the crops. They sung *"**Modimo wa Boikanyo**"* all the way and everyday.

They believed that people and all creation were created by God the Creator and that all shall return to God the Creator. They believed that God was in the highest holy place and that there is a holy communion of the ancestors immediate before the highest holy place. They believed that the ancestors are the living dead in the high holy place next to God. They believed that the ancestors will live, even though they die. They believed that the ancestors are watching over us wherever we are. They believed that the ancestors were in communication with God the Creator. They believed that God will give them what ever they ask from God in the names of their ancestors.

They were taught to respect their parents and all elders because one day they shall join the holy communion of the ancestors and communicate their needs and prayers to God the Creator. They revered God so high that they could not communicate their prayers directly to Godself. They revered a prayer so sacred that their knees trembled and they fell down on their faces and closed eyes and prayed God in the names of their ancestors. They knew that God is present, God is active and God is speaking to them through their ancestors in their sleep and when they are awake.

They believed that God can, and do, reveal Godself to people through dreams and visions; through life experiences; through prayers from the deepest chambers of their hearts; through miracles and through other people.

They knew and observed most of the Ten Commandments long before the Bible was written. They were born with intrinsic sense of what is right and what is wrong. They revered God the Creator; they honoured their fathers and mothers; they knew it was wrong to murder people; they knew it was wrong to steal; they did not commit adultery but married their beautiful women—one or more; they knew that man's cattle or donkey or piece of land belongs to a man and is his property; they knew that a piece of that land is that man; they knew that a human being is a human being because of other human beings; they loved one another and their neighbours and promoted peace.

King Moshoeshoe has never read a Bible but like Jesus Christ he promoted peace—**KHOTSO**—and still today his people greet each other with the words—**KHOTSO**—and still today his people welcome total strangers with the words—**KHOTSO**. Jesus Christ promoted peace up to the cross and back; and Moshoeshoe promoted **KHOTSO** up to the colonial borders and further that other side on the top of barren Rocky Mountains. Moshoeshoe and his people were driven from their beautiful rich land of Free State. A people of great suffering yet great dignity; a people who had so much to forgive, but who, in their generosity, do forgive; a people of hard work and committed hope for the future of their little semi desert.

There was a South Africa before 1652 and there were African people in South Africa before 1652. By then South Africa belonged to all South Africans. There was true peace and true conciliation and union of all South Africans because then the land and its wealth belonged to all South Africans. All South Africans had their fair share of land and its wealth. The land gave its people sustenance and better lives for all which ensured that Black people did not get extinct but continued to thrive from generation to generation.

The Motswana poet from passed generations tells us this about South Africa before the Whites: "*Nna pelo ya me ga e mo no sekgoeng. E kgakala kgakala fela kwa dikgweng. 'Fatsheng la Batswana. 'Fatsheng la bagale.'Fatsheng la dipula. 'Fatsheng la mabele. 'Fatsheng la dikgomo. 'Fatshe le 'kgomo tsa teng di gangwang di robetse.*" Simple translation: "My heart is not here in the White man's land. It is far, far away in the forests. It is in the land of my forefathers (he is Motswana). It is in the land of heroes. It is in the land of rains. It is in the land of corn. It is in the land of cattle. It is in the land where cattle are milked while they lie down." That is the South Africa of Black people before the arrival of a White man seen through the eyes of a poet in the olden days. It was South Africa of peace, prosperity, satisfaction and ease.

By then a Black man was a husband, a father, a keeper, a protector, a defender, a provider, a lover of life and beauty; not yet forced to be an accident of creation. The Black man walked tall without any fear, hatred or poverty assured of their inalienable right to human dignity—a people at peace with self, others and God the Creator.

The South Africa of before 1652 knew no wars because all Black people communities had enough land, cattle and wealth to lead satisfying quality lives. According to Jan van Riebeeck's report of 1660 to the Chamber of Seventeen in Holland; disputes and wars for land began in 1659; he writes: "The reasons advanced by the Africans for making war upon us last year, arising out of the complaints that our people had done them much injury, and also stolen and eaten up some of their sheep and calves, etc., in which there is also truth; so that they had cause for revenge, and especially, they said, upon people who had come to take and to occupy the land which had been their own in all ages, and keeping them off the ground, so that they must consequently now seek their subsistence by depasturing the land of other people, from which nothing could arise but disputes (wars) with other Black people."

Long before the Declaration of Universal Human Rights our people believed in the freedom and dignity of the individual human being. It is a fact that Jan van Riebeeck came with slaves from other parts of the world but our people helped these slaves to escape from Dutch farms and gave them refuge on our land. It resulted in the Dutch attacking our herdsmen for giving refuge to the escaped slaves from the new Dutch farms. That was in 1658 to 1660.

It is false that the White people found the Black people being heathens; satanic; barbaric; cannibalistic; backward; Godless; time-minded-less; unlearned; uncivilised and unable to think and unable to feel as people. That is why some White people still treat Black people worse than their pets and dogs in South Africa today. I do not dispute the widely published fact that we could not read and write; but as we were able to bring our different languages into existence, by now we could have on our own brought into existence reading and writing.

Long before our teachers came; it is a fact that somehow our foremothers could count the number of their own children. For a fact a husband knew the number of his wives. By the way, our self-appointed teachers had never bothered much to learn to speak, write or read our native languages. It means only one thing—which is—Black people taught themselves how to speak, write and read their own languages. No foreigner can teach people their own language.

Our lives were balanced around working the land and keeping charge of animals, wild and domestic, having time to play and teaching children fundamentals of life and loving life and loving selves and others. The Black people were contented.

If a man looses all his cattle through a misfortune or maybe lightning strike he was not lost and alone in the world. The entire village and the chieftainship suffered with him. It was a tradition that without asking for help his neighbours shall each loan him a cow or two—that is *dikgomo tsa mafisa tse digangwang go lebilwe kwa morago*. After five years his kraal is once again full of cattle and so he gladly returns back a cow or two to each of his neighbours. The debt is paid in full and all are happy and thus peace and reconciliation thrived for ages. That was before we could read the Bible that says love your neighbour as you love yourself. That was long before the Bible came to South Africa.

The human being was not lonely, insecure and fearful. It was long before the Whites came with: "Every man for him self". It was "Every man is only a man because of other men". It was the time of '*letsema*', when a man needed to extend his homesteads, the whole village volunteered to work and help him out of his problem. It was the epoch of 'the labour of love'. It was the time of '*kgetsi ya tsie e kgonwa ka go tshwaraganelwa; mabogo dinku a thebana*'.

Batsadi ba rona ga e sale ba itsile gore motho ke motho ka batho ba bangwe. We did not need funeral policies and death covers because it is against our culture for a person to dig his own grave or to plan his death and burial. All women came with comfort and something to eat wherever there was a funeral in the community. All men dug the grave at night and the next day there was a slaughtering of cattle and funeral was held. The skin of the cattle was used for entombment. That was before that fateful day of 1652.

Funeral was held within one or two days because all family members and relatives were present in the same village or in neighbouring villages. People of the neighbouring villages were also notified of the deaths of elders in a particular village. The slaughtered cattle were for catering visitors from neighbouring villages after funeral. There were no after tears. Only adults were allowed to attended funeral. Death and burial were not for children to hear about or talk about or even to see its procession. If there was a burial this side of the village children were sent to play that other side of the village. Children were not allowed to see the dead, not even their dead mother or father.

Death and the dead were respected to the level of almost being feared. Death was not common; it was for the great grand parents. Everything was done with dignity and prayers and praise songs of a particular clan were led by a clan leader or prominent person in the clan. Beautiful poems and laud poetic praises of the clan could be heard as the body was positioned in the grave.

By then it was our tradition and nature of life that children bury their parents, not parents burying their children as it is common today after 1652. By then our people could easily reach hundred years of age but could still walk and see and hear and tell stories to their great grand children. Their long life was connected to their good conduct and respect and to what they ate and drank. They mostly ate vegetables and fruits and corn meal and *sethathabola* and *maheu* and thick *inkomazi*. Milk and all kinds of meat were also in abundance.

There were no White man's hard drinks and drugs and tobacco. There was only a creamy *mtombozi* made out of rich *mabele* without yeast and other White man's ingredients. Instead of yeast our grandmothers used *tlhabego* prepared some days ago. Their lungs and livers and bodies and minds were not in for trouble as ours today.

Our ancestors lived a healthy lifestyle. There were no condoms and there was no HIV/AIDS and there were no many sicknesses and no sleeping around. There were no clinics and no hospitals, neither private nor public. Our culture demanded that a girl remained a virgin until she got married. A boy also remained untouched and waited until his parents presented him with a virgin wife usually from the same clan to marry. A boy and a girl could only be married after attending, completing and graduating from our traditional school.

It was a culture of Black people that a boy's family pays *lobola* to thank the girl's family for her good upbringing on the basis that she is still a virgin and that she will espouse the man's surname. After getting married the boy was no longer a boy but a man; after birth giving a girl was no longer a girl but a woman. There was no adultery but polygamy and there were no divorce court cases and no domestic violence because a man would always miss his wife after spending weeks with his other wives. And a wife would always miss her husband after weeks of rounds with other wives. Every time they meet it was hot and fire of love as the first time. Our lives were trouble-free, sweet and holy.

Polygamy was practiced for the mere fact that men were fewer than women, and most importantly, to protect the right of each and every woman to be loved and to have a husband, children and home. It was also to protect the right of each and every child to have a mother and a father. Not this common unbalanced single parent families. Polygamy was not a system of woman abuse but a duty of care and love provided and protected by each and every man. By then a Black man was a husband, a father, a keeper, a protector, a defender, a provider, and a lover of life and beauty.

There was no prostitution and no sex for sale. There were no prisons and no prisoners and no rapists and no murderers. Africans were together as one. Walking from another village in the dark of night a lonely walker was happy to meet people along the way. Today a person runs and hides away when he sees other people at night walking towards his direction. Before 1652 our lives were trouble-free, sweet, simple and at ease.

Before 1652 there were no currency and no debts in South Africa. South Africans needed not to work for any boss or any missies. There was no *baaskaap*. They needed no money and they needed no jobs. Please take note that the Setswana word for money is "*madi*". "*Madi*" is again a Setswana word for blood. I do not know why but I think and think. I think maybe the reasons are after 1652 (1). They were instructed to labour exhaustedly until they sweat blood to get little money and/or (2). They considered South Africa's currency to be "blood money" made from the spilled blood of millions of our people who were exploited and killed in the name of the economy and wealth.

I had the third reason but it refused to stick and fell off. My third reason was maybe money was as scares as blood but no, I was wrong. You will realise why as you read on.

Before 1652 there were no labourers, no workers, no servants and no servitude. All that was, was the labour of love. Men, women and children worked their own fields, livestock and homesteads on their own land out of their own will and love. Black people were the Masters on their own right; their own Masters. The African land and its wealth gave our great grand parents the right to be Masters. We are the children of the former Masters! Black children are the children of the Masters! They have the right to know that the great are only great because we are on our knees! They have the right to know because knowledge is power!

They must know that horrible accidents happened in South Africa after 1652. Historical accidents did occur! Historical accidents which were deliberate and were designed to put the destiny of a South African Black child in pain and agony forever.

Then there was no poverty and no million orphans. There were million cattle and million hectors of land. There was human dignity the meaning of which is freedom from fear, hatred, and poverty. There was no injustice and no colonisation and no apartheid. There was no landlessness, no homelessness, no street kids, no orphans, no hunger, no superior people, no lesser people, no wars, no prisons and no crime. Our lives were trouble-free, sweet, and holy and at ease; and the Black people were contented.

Before 1652 there were no borders of colonisation and no borders of apartheid. There was not even the First World War.

And then, 1652 came to South Africa. It came with the White people to a foreign but warm welcoming land and to its peace-loving and self-sufficient people.

The White people overtook the foot soldiers of Jesus Christ and landed in South Africa before them. Had the disciples of Jesus Christ arrived first, things could have been different.

THE LIFE IN SOUTH AFRICA AFTER 1652

The Whites arrived in South Africa as foreigners on 7 April 1652. They were warmly welcomed by the South Africans and given a piece of land to erect a tent to spend the night in. The explanation given to the Africans was that they were only taking a little rest then they shall continue their journey to the East. In the eyes of the Africans it appeared that Whites were only visitors to be given meal, water and accommodation based on ubuntu and African tradition.

They stayed the second day and night. They asked for a bigger piece of land to erect a bigger tent, which was given to them on the thought that they still needed more rest. During the fourth and fifth days the Whites explored the Cape. The Whites fell in love with the beautiful Cape and its glades and mountains and valleys. They fell in love with the deer and the springbok and sheep and cattle. They fell in love with everything African except Africans.

The Whites were truly enticed and madly in love with the Southern tip of Africa and so they decided to stay and settle forever. When they could no longer ask for more and more land, they demanded it. If their demand was not met they used forced removal of Africans from the African land. The Whites brought with them firearms and ammunition which were foreign to the Africans. African sticks and spears at that time were used only for hunting and were nothing compared to the destruction caused by the White people's ammunition.

On 10 February 1655 an early confrontation between the Africans and Whites takes place. Jan van Riebeeck writes in his Journal that when forced to vacate the land the Africans "declared boldly that this was not our (the White foreigners) land but theirs".

In 1658 the first war between Africans and Whites is provoked by Whites who forcefully settled in Liesbeeck Valley. Although brave the Africans lost the war because they had no weapons. The grabbed land is colonized with White settlers and used to produce wheat and wine grapes under Governor Simon van der Stel. My 'White name', Simon, originates from this 'White relative of mine'.

More and more Whites come from over seas in a rush to grab land. In 1699, in Simon van der Stel's memorial to his son, he observes that White farmers are pleading soil-exhaustion as an excuse to grab more land, where they only sowed enough for themselves and made a living by stock—barter: "Should you be weak enough to give way to such sinister tricks, the whole Africa would not be sufficient to accommodate and satisfy that class (of Whites)".

Land grabbing continues at a high rate. From 1715-1862 the Africans of the San origin have lost all their land to the Whites. They refused to give up the last piece of land they were standing on and it resulted on them being systematically exterminated to nearly extinction. Thousands are killed and a few escapes with nothing but the air to breath.

The badge of slavery; carrying of passes is introduced in South Africa in 1760 to control movement of the slaves in the Cape.

1779-1781 was the period of the first of a long series of so-called Cape-Nguni frontier wars, it consisted of cattle raids from the Africans. According to history books these cattle raids were mainly conducted by the Boers against Africans. But I think it could not be Boers only, I believe English people also joined on these raids. I think they were not mentioned to save the name of the Great Queen of England.

In 1795 the British occupy the Cape during the Napoleonic wars as the Dutch East India Company goes into decline. The Boers rebel against British rule and declare Graaff-Reinet and Swellendam independent republics. Both republics surrender when the British stop ammunition supplies to them.

In 1799 to 1803 the Khoikhoi, the San and the Xhosa drive a Boer commando and a British army out of the Suurveld.

In 1812 the army of British, Boer and Griqua troops expels the Suurveld's population of Africans, estimated at 22 000, eastward across the Fish River.

In 1813 the missionary John Campbell writes of a meeting with the Khoikhoi at their kraal south of the Orange River: "An old Hottentot told us that he remembered the time when the Boers were all within five days' journey of Cape Town, **and the country was full of African cattle;** but they have been driven up the country to make room for the White people."

In 1818 to 1819 the Xhosas are driven by the Whites as far back as the Kei River, with great bloodshed.

In 1820 the 4 000 British settlers are established near the eastern frontier.

In 1828 Ordinance 50, greatly resented by many Boers, is passed in the Cape, giving official recognition of ownership of land by Khoikhoi and other Black people.

Ordinance 50 did not stop land grabbing from the Black people.

In 1833 the landless Kgosi Seleka and his Batswana people (Barolong) were allowed to settle in Thaba 'Nchu by Morena Moshoeshoe.

In 1836 the Boers adopted the name "Africans" for their own identity. African in their language is "Afrikaner". Somehow this "African" brand name gave them great courage and determination to venture deeper into "their brand new" Africa—Afrika. Afrika en die Afrikaners. Hulle trek voor binne hulle Afrika, die Voortrekkers.

And so in 1836 the "White Africans" left the Cape.

The freeing of the slaves was their final grievance under the British rule in the Cape. A Voortrekker leader is later to write: "It is not so much their freedom that drove us to such lengths, as their being placed on equal footing with the Christians, contrary to the laws of God and the natural distinction of race and religion . . . wherefore we rather withdrew in order thus to preserve our doctrines in purity."

In 1837 Hendrick Potgieter's "White Africans" are attacked by Black Africans under Mzilikazi, the chief of the Zulus. The "White Africans" lost all grabbed cattle, sheep and horses to the original owner, Black Africans. They are left at loss and defeated.

The poor "White Africans" arrive in Thaba 'Nchu. The Batswana chief Moroka and his people welcomed them with great hospitality and ubuntu. They were given water, food and accommodation for sufficient time to rest and recover.

After the recovery of the poor "White Africans", chief Moroka of the Black Africans says to Hendrick Potgieter: "My fellow man I promise to help you and your people out of your suffering. I shall take my warriors and fight your battles against chief Mzilikazi."

Down and beaten the "White Africans" said: "Please, our Chief, if you do not go with us, doesn't make us leave this place".

Driven by compassion and empathy the Black Africans said: "We will go with you, and we will give you victory over Chief Mzilikazi, not once but twice".

And so it happened that the Black Africans accompanied the "White Africans" to punish Chief Mzilikazi both in Mosega battle and Egabeni battle. In both battles only Black Africans (Amazulu and Batswana) die. On the spilt blood of the Black Africans the "White Africans" were able to stand up again and re-grabbed cattle, sheep, horses and land from Black Africans—including from Chief Moroka and his Batswana people.

In 1843 the White Africans settled in "Trans Orangia", in Winburg district and Potchefstroom district.

The Aborigines Protection Society in London pleads that the Voortrekkers be prevented from wiping out the Africans. The Zulus are exterminated at the battle of Blood River by the Voortrekkers in 1838.

In 1839 the Voortrekkers settle in Natal. They resolve to drive out the remaining Africans from Natal, by persuasion if possible, by force if necessary.

In 1843 Britain annexed Natal.

In 1846 African reserves are established in Natal.

The same year of 1846 Sir Harry Smith appoints a Land Commission composed of White foreigners to give effect to his decision that several areas should be set aside for African use. The Land Commission reports that the majority of Africans in Natal are foreigners with no right to land. On that basis the Commission recommended that nearly all land in the country be allocated to Whites, not to Africans who are claimed to be foreigners.

In 1849 the Warden Line is created and leaves King Moshoeshoe and Basotho almost landless, with nearly all land grabbed to the benefit of Whites.

The same year 5 000 White men, women and children arrive in South Africa from England and Scotland.

In 1852 the Sand River Convention is signed and Transvaal Voortrekker Republic is given independence. Its original constitution states that: "The People desire to permit no equality between Africans and the Whites, either in Church or State."

In 1854 the Bloemfontein Convention is signed and OFS is given independence from the British rule.

In 1855 Sir George Grey rejects the policy of **apartheid,** then presented as a policy of territorial separation of the races. (NB! Re-surfaced in 1948)

In the same year the Cape Parliament amends the Masters and servants Act of 1842 to the favour of Whites.

In October of 1856 word goes out among the Amaxhosa for everyone to slaughter their cattle so that, following the prophecy of Nongqause, a great wind will sweep all Whites into the sea. Up to 200 000 cattle were killed as far west as the Fish River and as far east as Thembu land, and no crops were planted. By February 1857 there is wide spread famine; some 20 000 Africans die of starvation in Ciskei, while 30 000 migrate to White farms and labour for food. The great cattle-killing was an enormous disaster in the organised struggle of resistance against colonial rule in the Ciskei and against exploitation of Africans in White farms. The killing of the cattle was not an act of barbarism, but an act of expressing extreme desperation and agony suffered by Black people since the arrival of White people in Africa.

In 1860 to 1866 about 6 000 Indians arrive in Natal to work on the sugar plantation.

In 1861 the Boers move in to occupy Blood River Territory, claimed by the Transvaal under the Waaihoek Treaty.

In 1864 the Natal Native Trust is inaugurated—responsible for the locations of Africans. (NB! Extended to the whole South Africa in 1936)

In 1865 to 1868 chief Moshoeshoe is finally defeated by the Boers in a long and exhausting conflict. Moshoeshoe beaten and defeated and landless fled up the Rocky Mountains with the remnants of once a great prosperous peace loving nation. Britain came with help but it was too little too late. Moshoeshoe and his people lost the whole Free State to the Boers. Britain did not come to their rescue until they were driven totally out of Free State. Why did Britain wait so long and for such a great loss of life, land and property to happen first? And at long last Britain came rushing to annex the Rocky Mountains to become its colony and named it Basutoland.

In 1868 my great grandfather, Ntatemoholo Mohapi Mohapi, broke off from the fleeing King Moshoeshoe and his remnant people. My great grandfather fled in the opposite direction to that of the fleeing King Moshoeshoe; he fled towards Transvaal and settled in Leeudoringstad, then

Witpoort and lastly trekked to Khunwana in search of grazing rights. That is why today we find the Mohapi people in the then Transvaal and the then Bophuthatswana: Ha Mohlokalitse, Kraaipan, Ha Thulo-M'phete, and Diretsane. My great grand father and his Basotho clan were warmly welcomed by Chief Moshoette of Barolong in Khunwana and he gave them the liberty to settle in Kraaipan and the grazing land for their cattle in Mofufutso and then later Diretsane. Some of the Basotho people, the Bataung, welcomed by Chief Moshoette of Barolong were Sejake, Mohlamme, Shashape, Thulo, Mokoatsi, Sehloho, Kgalapa, Selepe, Mache, Makhoana, Molatudi, Madibo, and Mohapi of course. These Bataung were one people with common heritage and ancestry.

The diamonds are discovered in Kimberly in 1867.

In 1871 the Boer trekkers at Christiana insist that the Batswana chief Mankurwane of the Batlhaping pay taxes to them, but he refused, stating that he can not pay taxes to anyone in his land. This dispute results in a number of Batswana chiefs appealing to the arbitration court in Bloemhof on 04 April 1871. When the apartheid judges disagree on their verdict the matter is referred to Governor Keate, and on 17 October he delivers his judgment, the so called Keate Award, in which the land of the Batswana is defined as: "From the source of the Molopo River to the source of the Harts River to the source of the Makwassie River and along that river into the Vaal River in a westerly and southerly direction to Platberg Mountain; and then due west, touching the northern edge of the Langeberg Mountains. All land west of that line to the Kalahari is Batswana land."

This Keate Award did not help the Batswana people at all, not a bit. The Boers continued to grab their land at a high rate using superior force and ammunition; like in the Basotho land issue Britain did not come to their aid irrespective of repeated call of assistance and protection.

In 1874 to 1875 the Boer Republic of Transvaal expands westwards grabbing the Batlhaping, Barolong and Bakora land territories.

In 1877 the Boer Republic of Transvaal goes bankrupt. Its Boer force is defeated by the Bapedi. There is also a threat of Zulu invasion in support of Bapedi. The long held fear both in the hearts of the British and the Boers is awakened. The long-feared South African disaster, the concerted rising of the African people to "sweep the White man into the sea" (John Buchan). Britain acts decisively and quickly to protect the Boers by annexing Transvaal. It is the first step towards confederation—the union of South Africa.

In 1878 A. Trollope writes in his book "South Africa": "The Africans at Pretoria, and through all those parts of the Transvaal I visited, are an imported population—the Boers having made the land too hot to hold them as residents. The Boers hated them, and they certainly have learned to hate the Boers in return."

In 1878 and in fear of concerted Black Power uprising led by the Zulu, the Blood River Territory is given back to them.

The great Zulu King Dinizulu-ka-Cetywayo defeats the British at the Battle of Isandlwana in 1879.

In 1879 the Zulus are ambushed and exterminated in the Blood River Territory. This was done in order to crush the Black Power uprising possibility. The heroic mighty Zulu kingdom is weakened and broken up into separate chieftaincies. Their King is imprisoned. Both the Boers and the British are relieved by the defeat of the Zulu. The Boers occupy the Blood River Territory for the third time in 1881.

Strategically, after finishing with the Amazulu, the Whites proceeded to deal with the Xhosas. In 1880 the Ngqika-Xhosa Territory in the Ciskei is captured by the White farmers.

I think that is why my great grandfather reasoned that it was the British and Boers who caused wars and turmoil in South Africa, not the Africans. My great grand father usually differed strongly with the History I was taught at school. At school I was taught that it was the greedy barbaric Africans who caused unnecessary wars and turmoil in South Africa.

In 1884 the London Convention, to the complete disregard of the 1871 Keate Award, moves the Transvaal borders further west capturing Batswana lands.

I think that after realising that there is nothing to benefit from the barren Rocky Mountains of Basotuland in 1884, Britain pushed them from under her arm and declared them a "protectorate". Remember that Cape was British colony and Basotuland also was British colony. Why is Basutoland pushed away and not Cape? Why Cape was never declared a "protectorate"? Is Lesotho still a Protectorate?

In 1885 Britain decided to "protect" Bechuanaland in order to forestall the expansion of the German colony from South West Africa.

In 1885 Gcalekaland and Tembuland are grabbed into the Cape Colony, leaving only Pondoland independent.

In 1886 gold is discovered in Gauteng.

In 1886 there was an intention to annex British Bechuanaland to the Cape Colony. Chief Montsioa of Batswana addressing Pitso said: "I, Montsioa, tell you that I do not want the Government of the Cape. I now ask the Great Queen of England, with great earnestness no to give us over to Cape Colony, for if she does that she throws us away. If we remain under the Government of England, we live, I and my people. We shall not be divided into small locations."

During the same Pitso, the heir-apparent, Kebalepile Montsioa states in his speech: "The Cape could see no unrighteousness in the deeds of the Boers who were exterminating us. They shot our people, some whose arms were broken or wounded, they finished them off. Our people could be here today had they been taken prisoners and attended to as they should have been. In actions such as this the Government of Cape saw no wrong. Their eyes were so blinded that they could not distinguish between right and wrong. We are now disturbed in mind, and will not be at ease until the Queen has written us a letter to say that she will not hand us over to the Cape, and to say that we shall forever remain hers. If she does this we shall be filled with gladness, and we shall greatly thank the Great Queen of England."

The plea of the Great King and his great people did not get the favour of the Great Queen of England. They were sadly annexed to the Cape Colony in 1895. And still they sang "God save the Queen".

In 1889 the Superintendent-General for education in the Cape writes: " . . . to recognize the position of European colonists as holding paramount influence, social and political."

At this point in the History of South Africa it was apparent that the Black people have lost social and political power to the Whites but they still held on to their economic power. They still held on to more than half of the land and its wealth.

The Whites needed lots of people to work on their factories, mines and farms. The Black people were not available for that because they still had own lands and farms and livestock. The Whites got workers from over seas, like China and India, but it was only a drop in the ocean. It led into Whites doubling up their efforts to push Black people into agony, despair and submission into the position of inferiority.

In 1894 Pondoland was annexed by Britain into Cape Colony.

Mohandas Ghandi forms the Natal Indian Congress in 1894.

In 1896 to 1897 was a period of Batlhaping Rebellion at Phokwana (Langeberg). Rebellion was the results of their ten thousands cattle being shot and killed after being deceived that all cattle including that of their neighbouring White farmers shall be killed because of the epidemic. After the White police extinct their cattle, the neighbouring White farmers' cattle are spared. The Batlhaping people protested and it gave the Whites an excuse to turn the barrels of their rifles and cannons at them. The whole big settlement of Phokwane was destroyed and erased off the surface of the earth. The White police and hired White convicts and criminals pursued after the Batlhaping people as they ran for their lives. Ten hundreds escaped with nothing but the air to breath.

White people were recruited to South Africa, good and bad; free or convict. They were needed in big numbers so that they could occupy the land still occupied by the Black people. And so the convicts and criminals that helped in the kill at Phokwana were thanked with big farms on the land of Batlhaping. Captured Batlhaping, including women and children, were distributed around southern Cape farmers and forced into unpaid labour.

Paul Alberts, a White man, writes in his book that the head of one of the Batlhaping leaders was taken by a colonial official as a souvenir.

In 1897 the new colony of Zululand is incorporated into Natal.

In 1899 Black people were arrested for walking on pavements (sidewalks). They must compete with horse carts and cars in the middle of the road.

1899 to 1902 was the Anglo-Boer War. Black people were forced to fight on both sides of the war. Both sides promised them freedom from the weight of oppressive domination of either Boers or British rule. They fought for Boers and they fought against Boers. They fought for the British and they fought against the British. At the beginning of the previous century it was apparent that the Black people have been reduced to nothing but tools in the hands of White people.

My grand father survived the war to tell the story: "Hundreds thousands Black people were exterminated on both sides of the war. We were caught in the middle and at times I thought that both sides planned that war to finish us off."

"*My kind, daar die drie jaar oorlog was die slegte ding vir die swart mense. Ho ne ho tshabeha; ho le hobe ho swa motho!*" Tears come to his eyes and he abruptly stops and walks to the kraal to look at the new born calf.

After sometime he comes back and continues: "For three years without stop, cannons and all firearms in the world were finishing off the Black people. People ran helter scatter for dear life. Our village was swept off the face of the world towards sunset and I lost my father and my mother and my dear beloved first wife who was heavily pregnant and could not run. My parents were too old to run for their lives and my father cried out: "Run my son, fly; so that tomorrow you can make it right for our souls to rest in peace. Fly my son fly, so that you can live to tell about this day to the world and to your children and grandchildren. Quickly kiss the hands of your mother and wife for their blessings; do not hold them, do not kiss your wife on the lips for you might waste time. Do not worry about us because by knowing the day of our death makes your wife, your mother and I, better people than the rest. Now come for my blessings and go in peace my son."

"I was my father's thirteenth child and his most beloved child; the last born. I ran and stopped at a safe distance to look back. I saw my father with his spear and shield emerging from the homestead and making big strides towards the approaching blood thirsty Whites. Tall and huge lion of a man he was. He chanted a war song and bravely charged at them. I heard a loud bang and my father fell down never to rise up again. They jumped his body and hurried into his door yard. They ransacked my father's homesteads and lastly they came out with my mother and my wife from hiding.

The screams of my dear mother and my beloved young wife still pierce my heart as they were butchered cruelly to save ammunition. The woman of my father's cattle was the most beautiful person I have ever seen. I affectionately called her Queen Victoria and I loved her everyday up to today and every night I . . .-" I could not hear; the words become one with the cry of the old man.

After observing these wicked cruelties and annihilation of Black people, Joseph Chamberlain informs the House of Commons in London that: "The treatment of the African people has been disgraceful; it has been brutal; it has been unworthy of a civilized power (or people)". This means that the White people committing these hideous crimes against humanity are unworthy and wrong to claim that they were civilized and unworthy to claim that they brought civilization to South Africa. According to Chamberlain it was unworthy of civilisation. But, a naked killing and grabbing of people, their land and wealth.

In Sol Plaatje: Selected Writings, Brian Willian writes: "In many ways Plaatje's siege diary . . . has unique importance. In shedding light on the part played in the siege it explodes the myth, maintained by belligerents, and long perpetuated by both historians and the popular imagination, that this was a white man's affair: from Plaatje we hear not only of the experiences of the African population during the siege, the hardships they suffered and the difficulties they faced, but of their contribution . . . and the exploits, for example, of the famous Mathakgong in his many expeditions across Boer lines."

About the war Sol Plaatje writes: "We hear folks are eating horseflesh in Kimberly. We are not eating any just yet and pray for the war to end before we have occasion to do so. They are not shelling (killing) us as nearly as much as they used to do before".

It was the age of blood and conquest, the time in search and grabbing of gold and diamonds, land and glory. It was the epoch of accumulating wealth and prosperity at the price of killing Kings and Chiefs, and destruction of their communities and reducing them into servants.

It was the era of turning the rich and wealthy free nation of Black people into bondage, poverty, hatred and fear. It was the age of grabbing livelihood and prosperity from the Master people and turning them into the working class.

It was the time when the Masters were coerced into submission with the barrel of the gun to become Servants. Today, hundred years later, it is the time for the children of the former Masters to change the status quo or to remain servants and live in poverty forever. Now is the time to change the status quo to attain better life for all the children of the former Masters of South Africa!

Now is the time to break the unbroken chains of colonisation and apartheid! Now is the time to allow the martyrs and butchered people in the cause for freedom and equality to rest in peace! Now is the time to recover the lost struggle! Now is the time for true change and true peace and true reconciliation! Now is the time for our government to eradicate poverty!

1904 The war is over and yields nothing good for the Black people but much more agony.

1904 Black people must no longer stay in towns—"Towns are special places of abode for the White men, who are the governing race . . ." (Blue Book of Native Affairs; 1904).

1905 Black people must no longer stay in their rural places—"The mixed rural population should be abolished to create absolute social and political distinctions." (The Native Affairs Commission; 1905). 1906 Chief Sekgoma of the Batswana ba ga Tawana (Batawana) is deposed. arrested, and detained without trial for five years by the British colonial authorities.

1907 Black people to be exploited to the extreme,—"The defects of an uneducated man are balanced by the ease with which, owing to his simplicity and ignorance, he can be exploited as an economic asset." (The Christian Express; 1907)

1910 Black people are tight not to do crop farming and cattle farming freely and independently.

1911 Black farmers are reduced to doing farming on the system of farming-on-the-half, i.e. the system whereby Africans who own their own ploughs and oxen, enter into a partnership with the neigbouring White farmers, sow their own seed, reap the crop, and then hand over half of it to the White farmers in return to the right to cultivate, graze stock, and live in South Africa, "the land of a White African man".

1911 Against all odds, Black people can still do without becoming the working class for the White people. Black people resisted that class for many years.

1911 An angry White farmer in short of working class people, writes in the Farmers Weekly: "The sooner a gallows is erected to hang those who work on shares with the Ks the better."

1912 At a meeting of Cape Peninsula Native Association in Cape Town, about Blacks working in White farms, T.H. Mobutha stated that: " . . . And when their hard labour had made them physical wrecks, old before their time, they are turned adrift to starve."

1912 The South African Native National Congress is founded. Today is known as the ANC and today it is in the last double digit of years.

1913 The Native Land Act is passed and its negative far-reaching consequences are still suffered by the Black people today. Its immediate effect was to uproot millions of Black people from their land and farms and to send them wandering round the roads of their country seeking a place to live on. The White farmers could take them back on land only if they were prepared to labour for him. He could chase them out anyhow anytime. They worked for a little piece of land to stay on and for poorest quality of food, in "White" South Africa.

At long last, most effective than the guns and cannons; the Native Land Act of 1913 eliminated the perennial problem of labour shortage and finally turned Black people into the working class. Today Black people are 98 years old as the working class (or people) for White people in South Africa. I wonder if they are going to organise celebrations or mourning's for 100 years in 2013. According to Sol Plaatje the 1913 Land Act "empowers the government to expropriate our land by force to the benefit of Whites".

1914 A deputation of the ANC makes representations against the Native Land Act to the Colonial Secretary and the British House of Commons but the Whites did not listen. Britain did not help.

The same body sends a petition to King George V which states, abridged: "We are not against White people getting fair share of our land, but protest most strongly and solemnly against being squeezed out from land and squeezed out of rights to land." Again Britain did not listen and did not help.

The first President of the ANC, Rev. J.L. Dube petitions Prime Minister, abridged: "The South African Blacks have never suffered an act of greater injustice than the Land Act of 1913. We have seen our people driven from the places dear to them as the inheritance of generations, to become wanderers on the face of the earth." And still no help.

About the question of land and the new Land Act, Sol Plaatje writes: "Awakening on Friday morning, 20 June 1913, a South African Black man found himself not actually a slave but a pariah (a foreigner) in the land of his birth." Britain did not help.

The hidden aim of the Land Act was to reduce the Black people to a status of permanent workers for all purposes and for all times for almost no pay. The other hidden aim was by gradual process and by artificial means to reduce them to a status of permanent lesser people to Whites. It was a must that Blacks must always get half or far less of what they need. It was designed to forcefully submit the Blacks into the state of permanent lack and inferiority, and on the other hand it was designed to exalt Whites to the state of permanent wealth and superiority. And even today, in 2011, the status quo still remains. Please note that this was long before the introduction of apartheid policy in South Africa.

The aim was to reduce the Black people to a position of utter hopelessness, powerlessness, helplessness, defenselessness, landlessness, and homelessness; a condition of deepest humiliation and absolute dependency.

1914 to 1918 is the period of the first war in the world; World War 1. In this war once again Black people were used as tools after being misled to believe that it is a war of redemption from colonisation. The war was fought for more colonisation with the help of colonised people. It was one of those bitter ironies of the WW1 that colonised people had to pay such a high price for their own extra enslavement.

1919 The ANC deputation goes to Versailles in the expectation that the loyalty during World War 1 will be recognized "in some spectacular form or other." No help.

1920 Poor Whites in Vrededorp, Johannesburg, clash with Africans whose residence in their midst is no longer desired.

1921 The Native Affairs Commission reports that the town is a White area in which there is no place for Africans.

1922 The Stallard Commission reports that the co-mingling (staying together) of Black and White in towns must be stopped. Blacks must be thrown out of towns.

1923 J.C. Smuts states: "The Native Question is so large. We know so little about it; we know so little about certain factors which seem almost beyond human control."

1924 The White Pact Government adopts a policy of deployment to save the Whites out of poverty. There were many poor Whites. In most cases Africans are retrenched and Whites deployed to take their jobs.

1925 Corruption is rife in the White illegitimate government of South Africa.

1926 Hertzog's legislation which clearly establishes the principle that the Government and wealth of South Africa must be in White hands forever and ever.

1927 An Immorality Act is passed in Parliament to prohibit sexual intercourse between Black and White people. They must not stay together they must not love one another or make love.

1928 Councillor Qamata of Xalanga in the Transkei says in the Council: "The policy of the Government is to have two nations in South Africa. The natives (however) desired to be regarded as one nation with the White people."

1929 Hertzog declares South Africa a "White man's land." This implied that African people are foreigners in South Africa. Mahabane asked: "How can Africans be foreigners in Africa? Only uncivilized racist Whites have the answer."

Z.R. Mahabane, once ANC president, prays during the ANC meeting in Free State: "God forbids that we, as human beings, made in your image, should permit other human beings, made in like manner, to abrogate to themselves a position of superiority over us."

J.C. Smuts states: "A Black man may come for a limited period every year to work for the White man, he must leave his wife and children behind. Migration of his wife and children to farms and towns (White man's land) must be prevented."

In 1929 the strategy was then to destroy the very innermost fiber that gives people a human face; to destroy the family unit; separate a husband from his wife; separate children from their parents through labour migration. The Whites have long succeeded to destroy unity of the community life of the Black people and dispersed them over the face of South Africa as labour units.

In 1929 they failed to prevent women and children from migrating to farms on the trails of their husbands and fathers. Please note that it was only after 1994 that wives and children were removed from farms. Fathers were also removed because today in 2011 are forced to travel long distances daily between squatter camps and farms. They daily travel this long trying road in summer and winter at the back of open vans.

1930 Urban Areas Act excludes African women from towns.

1932 The Native Economic Commission states that a Black people's place must be "distinguished by sight, by its bareness"

1932 OFS Municipal Association describes Black people's places as "undoubtedly is that they are merely reservoirs for the purpose of supplying labour".

1936 Another Native Land Act is passed that fulfills the former.

1936 Committee on Native Education states that: "There is still strong opposition to their education because (1). It makes them lazy and unfit for manual work. (2). It makes him "cheeky" (3). It makes him turn against his culture and his people

1936 The process of grabbing the land from Africans continues.

1937 Police raid the Vereeniging location and Africans are wounded by rifle fire. The Police Commission of Inquiry finds "abundant evidence that the enforcement by the police of the present laws is often marked by unnecessary harshness, lack of sympathy and even violence." Remember how and why Andries Tatane was shot by the police three weeks back in Ficksburg. Are we not still ensnared by the cruel and painful history of our past? Such things must not have a room in the South Africa of true change and true reconciliation. I write this book so that we may know our painful past history to ensure that we do not repeat it.

1938 Dr D. F. Malan states to a new found nation of "Africans": "The battle of weapons is over. That was the Voortrekkers. But one, even more violent, more deadly than theirs, is being decided now. The battlefield has shifted. Your Blood River is not here. Your Blood River lies in the locations . . . The "African (Afrikaner)" of the new Great Trek meets the Africans (Black people) at their Blood River . . . defenseless at the open plains of economic competition." That is reducing Black people to beggars; they must always be in short of money so that they must never rise on the economic scale. Black people are pushed into poverty. That is why still today the Black people suffer and die in dire poverty.

1938 D.F. Malan is disturbed by the political dangers of a rising, educated class of Black people. They must not know because knowledge is power. They must be kept not knowing where they come from; ignorant of their past and history. Because an educated Black man wishes to share our way of life and strives for equality in all respect.

1939-1940 The Native Affairs Commission states that Black people locations are "reservoirs of labour" and congestion; land grabbing is welcomed as stimulant to the labour supply. Locations or municipal houses continue to be build.

1941 R.H. Godlo states in the Native Representative Council: "Today when a man is old he is kicked out of his municipal house because he can no longer pay rent. He has helped to build up your (the Whites) towns and economy, but in his old age you kick him out into the streets to become a doomed hobo."

1942 The Government committee investigating crime in Gauteng states that: "The wages of the Black people are so low which keep them chronically on the verge of destitution. Crime is a protest of the weak section from frustrated desires."

1942 It was common that Black people do not count as people. If an accident happens the news runs like "Two people are dead in the accident; one Boer, one British. And in the same accident 39 Ks have died."

1942 J.C. Smuts states: "When people ask me what the population of South Africa is, I never say it is two million. This country has a population of over ten millions, and that outlook which treats the Black people as not counting, is making the ghastliest mistake possible. If he is not much more, he is the beast of burden; he is the worker and you need him. He is carrying this country on his back." Today Black people reading these words would say: "Viva the spirit of Jan Smuts viva!" They would definitely consider him a friend of the people.

1944 Soweto is established.

1945 ANC adopts a Bill of Rights which demands an end to racial discrimination and equal citizenship for all people in South Africa.

1948 The new baby is born in South Africa and he shall be called Apartheid. He was conceived by the Whites and born from their womb but all his extreme agony is for the Blacks. Where were miscarriages? The settled permanent Black people in towns must be kicked out.

The National Party states: "The Black people in our towns must be regarded as 'visitors' who shall never be entitled to any political rights or to equal social rights with the White people."

1949 Mixed Marriages Act. It would make you think that because it does not say 'Stop Mixed Marriages Act' it allows mixed marriages of different people. No, it prohibits that. Remember they prohibited mixed sexual intercourse in 1927.

1949 The Black people' education in schools must inculcate "the habit of doing manual work". This is from the Government Commission of 1949.

38 000 petty Black offenders are forced to leave Gauteng to work on farms. It was the most cruel prison system designed to do away with labour shortages on Boer farms. It was another version of slavery.

The ANC adopts militant "Programme of Action" planned by the Youth League.

1950 Major demonstrations are held by the ANC.

The Group Areas Act is passed, it allowed that Black people may be evicted from home or place of work ruff and tumble.

The Immorality Amendment Act is passed to remind people of that of 1927. Sexual intercourse is a problem. Maybe people enjoyed inter-racial sex or mixed sex very much and it was not good for the policies of apartheid.

Dr E.G. Jansen, the Minister of Native Affairs states that: "Black people's status is that of foreigners'.

1951 Dr H.F. Verwoerd states: "We must deliberately see to it that the whole of South Africa is not occupied by the Black people". The Bantu Authorities Act is passed; she is the mother of Bantustans and Homelands.

1952 The new pass laws (the badge of slavery) are passed. The Badge of slavery, the pass book, must be carried by all Africans, men and women, born in South Africa, South West Africa, Basutoland, Bechuanaland and Swaziland, on reaching the age of sixteen.

The Prime Minister and politicians were above the law and above the Courts. For example in the year in question, the Appellate Division; the Highest Court on land, declared the Separate Voters Act to be "invalid, void and of no effect", because it was passed by a procedure that took no account to the Constitution. The Prime Minister refused to accept the court decision and overruled the court by continuing to implement this Act.

On the 6th of April, thousand of Africans gather in Pretoria's location and pledge themselves as "an oppressed people" to carry on "relentless struggle" for freedom and equality as laid down by the ANC with the support of Indians and Coloureds political parties.

On 26 June the Africans, Indians and Coloureds launch a civil disobedience campaign, which reach its apex in October, and rapidly declines following violent government counteraction.

Influx control of Black people is toughened with the amendment to the Natives Act.

Large prisons outstations are built in direct response to shortage of labourers in Boer farms. Hundred thousands of Black people are picked upped for petty crimes and forced to provide free labour on farms.

1953 Dr H.F. Verwoerd comments on the new Bantu Education Act: "The Bantu must be guided to serve "his community" (should read "White people") in all respects. There is no place for him in the White community above the level of certain labour." This Act was passed explicitly to provide Black people with education for a subordinate position in South Africa as a whole.

He further criticises the former education system as having created a class of African which "feels that its spiritual, economic and political home is among the civilised White community of South Africa".

1954 The Native Resettlement Act is passed which provides for the removal of all Africans from towns and cities.

The government applies the principle of "divide and rule" in building of African townships and locations. It destroys the unity of African people by "ethnic grouping" in building of locations.

1955 The Congress of the People is established. SACTU—South African Congress of Trade Unions is also founded in 1955. On 26 June 1955 the Freedom Charter is adopted in Kliptown by about 3 000 accredited delegates. Among others it states that: "We, the People of South Africa declare for all our country and the world to know that South Africa belongs to all who live in it, Black and White, and no government can justly claim authority unless it is based on the will of all the people; that our people have been robbed of their birthright to land, liberty, and peace by form of a government founded on injustice and inequality". It further states that: "the restriction of land ownership on racial basis shall be ended, and all the land re-divided amongst those who work it . . . All shall have the right to occupy land wherever they choose . . ."

The Freedom Charter is the charter of a democratic South African nationalism, implicitly denying the concept of "Africa for the Africans". It also combines a bill of rights with such socialist aims as the transfer of mineral wealth beneath the soil (the mines), the banks and monopoly industry to the ownership of the people as a whole.

The government responds to the Charter by raids against the people, political arrest and the mass arrest on 5 December of 156 leaders of all racial groups in towns and villages throughout the country on charges of treason. 19 December marks the beginning of the so-called Treason Trial.

1956 About creating Bantustans and Homelands, Verwoerd states that: " . . . the opportunity of separate government, the opportunity of living separately . . . does not of necessity mean that the economic activities of the country should be split up".

1956 20 000 Black women march in Pretoria to present petitions protesting the extension of pass laws to women. Marching and chanting: "*Wa thinda umfazi, wa thinda umbokodo!*" "you hit a woman, you hit a rock".

1957 The uprisings of Black people in villages and rural areas begin and lasted up to 1962. The uprisings started in Tembuland, Transkei,

Sekhukhune land and Zeerust. These uprisings are a reaction to poverty, land deprivation and tension, heightened by the application of Bantu Authorities Act, the deposition of chiefs and the requirement that women carry passes. All these uprisings are suppressed with government brutality, especially in Pondoland, where military force, Sten guns and armored vehicles are used. Mass arrests are also carried out.

1957 The Native Laws Amendment Bill, with its notorious Clause 29 (c), the so-called "Church Clause", is introduced to parliament. It states that no Black people should attend church service in town without the permission of the Minister of Native Affairs. I wonder if the permission from the Minister to pray in town is still necessary, because even this year, every Sunday I see Black people travelling from towns to locations to attend church services there, not in towns where they live.

It was not desired that Black and White people should mingle equally and freely in churches, schools, hospitals, hotels, bars, clubs and other places of play and entertainment.

Uprisings take place in Johannesburg African townships, especially in Dube where more than 40 Africans are killed. It is reported that the riots are connected to the Treason Trial, ethnic grouping of Blacks and enforced migratory labour system.

1958 Shortly before the general election in April copies of a handbill, with a message to White voters from Chief Luthuli, President-General of the ANC, are widely distributed. Among others it said: "Never since Union of SA has our people suffered such hardships, humiliations and sheer brutality as we have had to undergo during the past ten years of the government of NP . . . our poverty has become desperate. Our leaders and spokesmen are arrested, banned, deported and silenced . . ." The message was a cry for help from the White people. It fell on deaf ears as the White voters voted again for the NP in great majority.

It becomes an offence for an African man not to posses a pass.

The government grabs the Onverwacht farm from 241 Black families who lived there for more than hundred years. After unsuccessful appeal they become homeless and landless.

1959 H.F. Verwoerd is the new prime minister and apartheid is put into the top most gear:

1. The Representation of Africans in Parliament is abolished

2. Eight Bantustans/Homelands for Africans are recognized

3. Commissioners-Generals are appointed to represent the government in Bantustans

4. The appointment of representatives (chiefs "ambassadors") of Territorial Authorities in urban areas

5. The establishment of a constitution and powers of Bantu Authorities

6. Prominent ANC leaders are banned as well as ANC meetings

7. Black children are not allowed to attend the universities without a permit from the Minister of Education

8. Formidable barriers against social relationships between persons of different races are raised

The urban riots of previous year continue.

Pan African Congress is established under the leadership of Robert Sobukwe. The PAC President was a lecturer in Zulu at the University of Witwatersrand. Potlako K. Leballo is elected the National Secretary of the PAC. Sobukwe states that the PAC rejects Apartheid and aims at the government of the Africans by the Africans, and for the Africans . . . and anyone who is prepared to accept the democratic rule of an African majority being regarded as African.

1960 It becomes an offence for an African woman not to posses a pass.

The revolts in rural areas gain momentum, especially in Pondoland. Journalists are refused permit to enter the African Reserves. Squads of heavily armed patrol the affected areas using helicopters and aircraft. Africans are killed by police to end the revolts.

Robert Sobukwe announces that the PAC has planned a campaign aimed at the abolition of pass laws, which will commence on 21 March. People are being called upon to leave their passes at home and to surrender themselves for arrest at the nearest police stations. The slogan "no bail, no defence, no fine" will be strictly adhered to. After serving their goal sentences, the people will offer themselves again for arrest. This was to be the commencement of no passes and arrest cycle that shall eventually make it unnecessary to arrest people on the basis of not carrying passes. It was to lead to the point where people shall no longer carry passes and police shall no longer arrest them because it was all useless. There was wisdom and good judgment in Sobukwe's call.

Phillip Kgosana, addressing the mass meeting in Langa on the day before the campaign started said: "This is not just another protest but the start of a new South Africa, in which all Blacks would finally unite to compel change. Every African had to promise himself that he would never again carry a pass. He quoted from Sobukwe's written message that: 'the campaign must be of ABSOLUTE NON-VIOLENCE. Allowing the campaign to degenerate into violence will be to alienate the masses by using them as a cannon fodder. After a few days, when we have buried our dead and made moving graveside speeches and our emotions have settled again, the police would round up a few people and the rest will go back to their passes. This is a never-ending stream of nonviolent campaigns until a goal of our freedom had been reached. We are not leading corpses to a new South Africa'."

But it was not to be. The 21st March came and the police came to shoot and kill the people. In Sharpeville 68 Africans are mercilessly exterminated and hundreds were wounded, including innocent children.

Joseph Lelyveld writes in his book 'Move Your Shadow': "It is possible to pinpoint an hour in which the Bastille might have been stormed in South Africa and wasn't. That prospect was raised, glimpsed, and extinguished on 30 March of 1960. On that morning, a possibly 30 000 Blacks marched in ranks down a highway that winds around the lower slopes of Table Mountain in Cape Town to the Parliament Buildings itself and offices of the white government. By the time the vanguard got that far, an air force helicopter was hovering overhead and armoured vehicles with police and army units were massing in the side streets. White troops with fixed bayonets arrayed themselves in front of Parliament, and machine-gun emplacements were established on its grounds. The White power was having a giddy feeling that it was rocking on its foundations. No one could calculate the possible repercussions of another Sharpeville at the portal of White power. If it did not amount to the fall of Bastille, it could hardly been a lesser moment in South African history than the storming of the Winter Palace in Russia. A notable feature of the march was the almost complete absence of ill-feeling. Schools were dismissed early on account of the presumed menace that the marchers represented. The rushing home colured school girl observed: "I had only one more street to cross," she said, "but that was the street the Ks (Blacks) were marching down. I was afraid to cross. I stood inside one of the shops and prayed to God that no one would say anything to upset them. The next day in school, some of the boys said they hoped that the Ks burned the whole Cape Town down, just to show the Whites." Where did the feelings of inevitability that the marchers obviously felt and inspired come from? And more to the point where did they go? The answers are on the relationship between that huge throng and its leader, who wielded authority that seemed absolute over thousands who might have been expected to dismiss him as a boy. Phillip Kgosana was the leader of the multitudes. He was slightly built, twenty three years old and only six years out of primary school. "When I told them to sit down, they sat down," he later testified when summoned as a witness before a White commission of inquiry. "When I told them to stand up, they stood up. When I ordered them to go back quietly, they went back quietly."

For a period that can be measured in minutes Phillip Kgosana, a student wearing shorts, appears to have held the fate of South Africa in his hands as no other single man has done before or since. There can be no doubt that if he had ordered the multitudes to storm the Parliament, they would have stormed it, whatever the consequences. It was the matter of just saying the words: "Hit at the police, take their firearms and storm the Parliament!" What stopped him from saying the word: "*A e hlome e hlasele!*" still remains unanswered.

After Kgosana ordered the multitudes to disperse peacefully, the trembling Whites hurriedly proclaimed the state of emergency on the very same day. The Whites nearly lost it all to the Blacks and so no further chances should be taken. This state of emergency continued for decades. All parties and organizations are banned, including marches and peaceful protests, gatherings and meetings. Black people were not allowed to be more than five at a time, then it was illegal gathering or illegal meeting and they were arrested. In a number of days 18 011 people were arrested.

1961 The era of non-violence by the Blacks is over and 'Umkonto we Sizwe' take over from the unarmed masses of the people. The brave Nelson Mandela called it the "Spear of the Nation". The era of the ANC led armed struggle dawns in South Africa. The intellectual Oliver Tambo reasoned that the arm struggle is imposed on Blacks by the violent government of South Africa.

Britain for the first time condemns apartheid and votes against it in the UN.

Verwoerd states that in the light of pressure being exerted on South Africa he encourages the advancement of African Homelands and Bantustans and will think the granting of independence to them. This must ensure that the White man retains freedom and his right of domination in what is "his country".

Referring to the eventual independence of Transkei, the Minister of Bantu Administration states that as long as there are Whites in the towns of Transkei their affairs will be controlled by the White government. The Bantu will rule their own people only.

The Batswana Territorial Authority comes into being under the leadership of Chief Tidimane Pilane. He is reported as saying that all people with self-pride want independence.

The government grabs the land owned by the Bahurutshe tribe near Zeerust since 1894. The land owned by Africans in Boomplaats was also grabbed in 1960 by the government.

1962 The Department of Bantu Administration and Development employs Africans to build the Ga-Rankuwa Township, later to become part of Bophuthatswana, for the housing of industrial workers at Rosslyn, near Pretoria.

1962 The government appoints Chiefs for the Black people to implement government's agenda in Bantustans and Homelands. The government disposes Chiefs who refuse to collaborate with apartheid policy. Maybe the government does not know that a Chief like a King is not appointed but born.

The government decides it has no choice but to regard the Indians as citizens of South Africa because it has failed to repatriate them and also failed to create 'their own little India' in South Africa. It also decides that Coloureds are citizens of South Africa. It is only Africans who are closed out as foreigners in South Africa and the government had to create for them 'their own little Africa's in South Africa'.

1963 Transkei becomes the first official Homeland, "*the first of many future independent African states in one and many South Africa*". It sounds as total madness but that is how Verwoerd and his gang saw it and that is how it came to pass.

The Minister of the Interior reports that there were still 438 "Black spots" on the "White face", meaning Black people settlements in South Africa.

Chief Mampuru is found guilty of defying an order to move with his Bapedi people from Hlakudi and is fined.

1964 Verwoerd states that: "The mere presence of larger number of Blacks in employment does not mean integration. It is only when there is intermingling of them in social, political and religious lives that one really gets integration. The mere fact that Blacks as foreigners are employed in a community or in other country does not constitute integration."

During the Rivonia Trial, the brave Nelson Mandela states that because all other means of opposing apartheid had been closed, leaders of Umkhondo we Sizwe had decided to organise sabotage. They chose sabotage as weapon rather than terrorism.

The government introduces Bantu Laws Amendment Bill to ensure that Black people remain in a permanent state of fear, insecurity and poverty as long as they live. There is almost a total denial of them being human beings and individuals. Each one is simply reduced to interchangeable labour unit.

Helen Suzman of Progressive Party states that the Bill "strips the African of every basic pretension that he has to being . . . a free human being in the country of his birth, and it reduces him to the level of a chattel".

1965 Verwoerd states that: "I believe in the supremacy of the White man over his people in his territory, and I am prepared to maintain it by force". Even in their independent Countries, Homelands and Republics the Black people shall remain under the control of White South Africa.

G.F.L. Froneman states in parliament: "Black people are only supplying a commodity, a commodity of labour. It is labour we are importing and not labourers as individuals. Numbers make no difference."

Despite the wealth of South Africa hundred thousands Black children do not get education because there are very few schools.

Nearly 100 000 Black men and women are "endorsed out" of towns.

The influx control cause terrible hardships for Blacks. One example in millions:

Old man Sobekwa and his wife had eight children. He is partially incapacitated following an accident in the mines in 1949. The old man and woman are supported by their older children. One night during the influx control the old man and old woman are arrested on their sleep. The court finds that old Sobekwa has long forfeited his right to remain in Cape Town because the court claims that he was away for a year in 1957 (he denies this), the grand parents are forced to serve prison sentences. When the grannies are released from prison they find out that they no longer have home or no children. Their children have long been 'endorsed out' and their house given to hostile people. They are forced to become helpless hobos. You might think that there was a prize for the highest number of hobos produced by government officials.

1966 The Black people shall be faced by restrictions in South Africa because they are in another people's country. This fallacy point was made by H.F. Verwoerd, the Prime Minister.

1966 September, H.F. Verwoerd is stabbed to death on the front bench of the White Parliament by a parliamentary messenger. Unfortunately this time around his life could not be saved and preserved for the White nation like on previous occasion. It was previously successfully preserved after two bullets had been fired into his head by a would-be white assassin. Lelyveld, in his book, states: "I never got closer to Hendrik Verwoerd than the press gallery in Parliament, from which I would watch him as he contemplatively fingered the scar that one of the bullets had left next to his eye."

Joseph Lelyveld writes: "I never suspected that much of what I took to be the temper of Boers is derived from the temper of Hendrik Verwoerd, a self-made "African" who had been born in Amsterdam before he immigrated to South Africa." Arriving in the aftermath of Anglo-Boer War, Verwoerd's family had tasted none of its bitterness. But those who could never forgive or forget took him and made him their leader. It was Hendrik Verwoerd who finally led them out of the Commonwealth, reviving the legacy of the Boer republics which were crushed when he was an infant in Holland. Verwoerd had no tolerance for disagree, no tolerance even for tolerance. As a result, disagree voices of Boers against Apartheid were nearly zero. In his mind there was a plan, *and it was moral and it would work:* The Africans shall be in their "motherland/fatherland" "Homeland/Bantustan", and all will be right with the world. He sounded reasonable because he spoke in syllogisms. He said: "It is evil and cruel to deny Black people their human rights by allowing them to live in our 'vaderland'. They belong in their countries, *nie Suid Afrika nie*. I shall create for them their own countries, *nie in Suid Afrika nie*, but in their Homelands." When he was done, the Boers went home smiling and congratulating him for his Christian generosity; God-send mans, *not* this immigrant son of an immigrant. From that day onwards Africans were regarded as immigrants in Africa from nobody knew. Their movement was restricted by the passing of severe pass laws.

On average 1 313 Blacks are arrested daily under the pass laws.

Lorries are sent to move African people from Holpan to Mamuthla. They are allowed to take with them removable materials from their dwellings. On arrival in Mamuthla the Africans find that no tents have been erected for temporary shelter, no rations are provided, no water supply, and no work is available locally. (Others were dropped in Majeakgoro, 80 kilometers away from Holpan)

1967 The Minister of Labour states that: "Africans have no right of existence in the Western Cape, which is the natural labour field of Whites and Coloureds."

Chief Tidimane Pilane, chairman of Batswana Territorial Authority, states that he envisages Bantustans/ Homelands eventually combining to form one great Black state.

The government lays down three categories of Africans who can be removed from the "White man's land" to the Homelands: (1). The elderly, the unfit, widows, and women with dependent children. (2). "Surplus" Africans on White-owned farms, on mission stations and on "Black spots".

Specials townships (one-roomed dwellings) are build in Homelands to accommodate Africans from the Western Cape. For example, 3 000 Africans are settled in Sada at Shiloh, near Whittlesea in the Ciskei. They are forced to move from living in big houses to live in corrugated iron and asbestos one room per family. No work is available at Whittlesea, and they are not allowed to take up employment in Queenstown. There are no trees or other fuel, no clinics or resident doctor. Thirty three people die there during the first six months of 1966, two of old age and the rest of various diseases.

At that time Transkei could only employ 32 700 people excluding professionals and teachers. This is according to "Annual of the Transkeian Government for 1966".

1968 The Transkeian Government asks Pretoria to prepare Transkei for independence in the shortest possible time.

The Batswana Territorial Authority is reconstituted and Chief Lucas Mangope becomes its first Chief Councillor.

The Department of Bantu Administration starts actively persuading other "nations" to form their own "Republics".

Thousands of Africans are removed from their farms in Meran to Limehill under appalling circumstances. They are given about three days notice that they are going to be moved, and when the lorries arrive they are forced to leave behind their cattle and other livestock. At Limehill tiny yards have been demarcated. The preparations are inadequate. There is no sanitation or firewood, no school, no clinic, and no water. The people are expected to live in tents not yet pitched. Many people have furniture which they are unable to fit into the tents. It is raining, oh, what a destruction of property and people. Forced removal from land was also aimed at the total destruction of Black people's lives. Apartheid celebrated in the suffering and agony of Black people.

A "Black spot" near Glencoe, called Boshoek, is a farming area of the Kunene people since 1870. Nearly 5 000 Africans lived there. Their land has plenty water and grazing. Their land and livelihood are grabbed from them by the government. They are resettled against their wishes at Vergelegen, about 6 km from Limehill.

The Moletestad of Bakubung, near Rustenburg, since 1890 is ordered to move to Ledig. The people resist, but after the government demolished a school, the people are induced to move. However, 180 families still refuse to leave, and are charged and sentenced to fines or imprisonment.

Bakwena Ba-Mogopa were ordered to leave their farming land of Swartkop, near Koster, to make way for White diamond diggers. The Bakwena moved here when they broke off from the Basotho of Moshoeshoe in 1866 in the OFS. They have made many improvements on the land since then. The Bakwena people were forced to disperse through out South Africa. Today some of Bakwena, the Mahupela, Kgabi, Kgantsi, Tudi, Taje, Molefe, Tsoku, Monnye, Mosia, Melamu, Mmusi, and Leaje are strangers to each other as if they do not come from the same house and common ancestry. Some of these Bakwena are today found in Middleton, Manamolela, Atamelang, Marotse, Kopela, and Diretsane.

1969 The Bantu Homelands Citizenship Bill is introduced. It provides that there will be separate citizenships for each Homeland.

1970 The White farmers press for the forced removal of million Africans near Lesotho border, since this cover vital watershed.

White miners protest against the government's plan for the gradual advancement of Africans in the Homelands and refuse to train African miners. The Minister of Mines gives some assurances to them: "No White miner would lose his job, and no White miner would be placed under the authority of a Black miner. If, in time, the same work is done by some Whites and some Blacks, it would be carried out in separate shits or separate sections of the mine."

643 897 Africans are arrested for infringements of pass laws in the year ending 30 June 1970.

1971 Chief Gatsha Buthelezi, CEO of the Zululand Territorial Authority states: "Homeland leaders who have accepted separate development have done so because it is the only way in which Blacks in South Africa can express themselves politically."

Chief Gatsha Buthelezi to the Sunday Times, states: "Great human tragedy is unfolding: thousands of evicted Zulus from land are wandering homeless—a great Black trek—preferring to keep on the move rather than lose their cattle."

433 Batlhaping families at Majeng under Chief Jeffrey Moseki, are instructed to leave their land, and to move to a farm called Vaalboshoek. Chief Moseki resists. He is arrested with other five senior members of the Batlhaping. The government sent in bulldozers to demolish the houses of Batlhaping.

After many hardships and long resistance, a group of Barolong people at Machaviestad near Potchefstroom, are finally resettled at Rooigrond, near Mafikeng. There is no land for ploughing, no schools or clinics, no work available locally, and social pensions have not been paid since they moved.

615 075 Africans are arrested for offences under pass laws.

1972 Instead of Chief Tidimane Pilane, Chief Manyane Mangope becomes the Chief Minister of Bophuthatswana. Be reminded that Chief Tidimane Pilane was not that compromising to the apartheid policy. His thinking was in the near future to unite these Homelands into one big mighty Black state of South Africa.

Zululand changes its name to Kwazulu.

Jerry Modisane, President of SA Students' Organisation says in an interview: "We do not need the co-operation of the White man anymore—and we do not want him. We can find liberation from perpetual servitude on our own."

B.J. Vorster states: "English language newspapers should not incite Black leaders in the Homelands to ask for more land".

Chief Gatsha Buthelezi states: "The 1936 land proposals are not realistic in terms of offers of independence or in terms of population figures".

Prof. H.W.E. Ntsanwisi, Chief Councillor of Gazankulu, states: "The policy of separate development is generating insecurity, uncertainty, and frustration . . . As it is now, we have no final say. Decisions are made for us, and not by us."

Chief Lucas Mnagope reaffirms his support for the *positive* aspects of the policy of apartheid. He states: "To brand my colleues and me as Government stooges reveals a misconception . . . It is true I don't believe in confrontation. But I also believe in speaking my mind, whether this is acceptable to Pretoria or not."

Chief Tidimane states: "I accept the policy of separate development only because of the implied promise that the Batswana will regain the land of their forefathers and will achieve sovereign independence."

Chief Lucas Mangope says at the University of Stellenbosch: "I believe in separate development as long as the promised sovereign independence does not mean an eternal provincial status for a Homeland, but where the foundations are laid in such a wholesome way that its citizens are enabled to aspire to that sense of self-respect. I want to give the assurance that I do not consider the Whites as settlers, as foreigners, or as squatters, or temporary sojourners in this country. By the same token I cannot accept that these labels be attached to my people. The very idea of White representation in Parliament for Blacks is an insult to any self-respecting Black."

An average African old-age pension is R5. The Rev. David Russels (a White man) protests for six months against it by deciding to live on it and by writing open letters to the Minister describing his experiences; physical and mental conditions. These letters are published in the Press.

1973 Chief Gatsha Buthelezi is against the apartheid policies and says that its policies are totally unacceptable to the Zulu people. He says that his government will not co-operate in the proposed further removals of Africans from land.

Chief Lucas Mangope rejects the Government's revised 'semi plans' for the consolidation of Bophuthatswana. He produces his own plan which doubles the size of Bophuthatswana.

A summit meeting of Homeland leaders is held in Umtata. The leaders decide in principle that a future federation of Homelands in South Africa is vital to the unity of Black people. Chief Lucas Mangope, however, states that he still has the feeling that a federation with Botswana might be more in the interests of Batswana.

Chief Gatsha Buthelezi tells the crowd of Africans who gather outside the hotel where the summit is held, that none of the architects of separate development could ever have dreamed that their policy would be used as a platform on which to build Black solidarity.

1974 Chief Lucas Mangope says at the Conference of Race Relations in SA: "To talk about the political future of the Homelands is to talk about the political future of SA, even more correctly, of southern Africa. The Homelands are a reality, and a reality with which we must learn to live. Whether it was wise to create them has become irrelevant . . . There must be a more just and fair sharing of land. "

About the economy Chief Mangope says: "There is failure to induce a significant shift of the market across the borders into the Homelands. Though the workers will sleep in the Homelands, they will continue to spend much of their earnings in the White area . . ."

Africans continue to be removed from their lands and farms and to be dumped in Homelands, Mangope writes to Pretoria: "The removals are taking place without the consent and against the wishes of my government."

598 landowning Bapedi people are removed from their farm Doornkop, near Middelburg. They are forced to move without any compensation for their land as is usual to the treatment of Africans.

A daily average of 6 121 African prisoners worked for governments departments. A daily average of 18 142 African prisoners worked for private persons (and local authorities).

1975 Chief Gatsha Buthelezi releases to the Press a memorandum which he has read out to B.J. Vorster during his meeting with Homeland leaders. In this he says, *inter alia,* that unless the Homelands are enlarged and properly consolidated, the only alternative is for Africans to be represented in the Central Parliament. He also announces that the Prime Minister has rejected any possibility **of Soweto being declared a Homeland!**

The Bop. Democratic Party gives Chief Mangope a mandate to lead Bophuthatswana to future independence from South Africa. Chief Mangope promises that the independence would be used as a lever for bringing about political change and for ending racial discrimination in SA. On 19 November the Legislative Assembly agrees to start negotiations for independence.

1975 Inkatha Yakwazulu, 'a national cultural liberation movement' open to all Zulus is founded. Its name is subsequently changed to Inkatha Yesizwe.

Chief Geoffrey Mosehi of the Mayeng land encourages his people to resist resettlement scheme. When officials arrived from Pretoria to continue with the scheme, they find the village of Mayeng deserted, all the inhabitants vanished. Pretoria went back with uttermost surprise. Then people came back to their village from hiding in the forest. Days later Pretoria came back unannounced and deposed Chief Mosehi and demolished his house.

1976 About land grabbing Chief Mangope says at the Graduate School of Business, University of Cape Town: "It is typical that the powerful . . . seem determined to bully or intimidate the powerless into submission. Our impotent anger and resentment . . . from the fact that the 1936 Land Act . . ."

B.J. Vorster: "There shall never be one-man-one-vote in South Africa. There shall not be a multi-racial conference."

1976 May 06, Desmond Mpilo Tutu writes a long detailed prophetic letter to Prime Minister, B.J. Vorster: " . . . I am writing to you, Sir, because I have a growing nightmarish fear that unless something drastic is done very soon then bloodshed and violence are going to happen in South Africa. A people can take only so much and no more. . . . A people made desperate by despair, injustice and oppression will use desperate means. I am frightened, dreadfully frightened, that we may soon reach a point of no return, when events will generate a momentum of their own, when nothing will stop their reaching a bloody denouement which is too ghastly to contemplate".

A month later Tutu's prophetic letter of violence erupting becomes a reality. June 16, the Soweto uprisings, the outbreak of violence and race riots on a large scale than has ever been experienced before in South Africa. According to figures released by the Police, in Soweto alone the Police had fired 16 000 rounds, killed 200 Blacks, and wounded 1 500 Blacks. Many were shot from behind.

Vorster refuses to discuss the uprisings with Homeland leaders and rejects to abolish Bantu Affairs Administration Boards viewed as "instruments of apartheid". Immediately after the meeting Chief Buthelezi tells the Press that "in the face of persistent White intransigence and the determination of Mr. Vorster, shown at the meeting with the Homeland leaders, to maintain White domination and apartheid, we have no alternative but to close ranks".

The same year of 1976, the Bakolobeng people of Kgosi Molete are forced to move from Ha Maloka farms near Lichtenburg to Gannalagte near Kopela and Diretsane. Ha Maloka has been the land of their fathers since 1870. The Bakolobeng also originate from OFS. They left OFS in 1866 after approximately 700 farms were expropriated from Black people by the Boers. Hundred years later they are dumped in a semi desert called Gannalagte, from the beautiful land of Ha Maloka. Ha Maloka was the land with tarred roads, windmills, rolling hills and valleys, water spring and ever running streams, clinic and schools, well developed fields and lands for sustainable farming and livestock keeping. There was vibrant life in Ha Maloka, with Lichtenburg town just around the corner. Then the people's lives were destroyed and they were moved to Gannalagte next to nothing; to start all over again.

OAU refuses to recognize Transkei as independent state.

The UN also refuses to recognize Transkei or any Homeland as independent state.

On 26 October 1976 Transkei becomes the first Homeland to gain its independence from South Africa.

1977 The very first meeting of a South African Black leader and President of USA takes place between Chief Gatsha Buthelezi and Jimmy Carter in USA.

Chief Lucas Mangope says at the National Congress of Coloured People's Party: "Like you I am a South African. Like you I am someone who passionately clings to his South African identity. Because I have always been a member of South African community, and shall always continue to be, regardless of those in the seats of power classify me. No one can decide that I am suddenly no longer what I am and shall continue to be until my death. We have recently experienced the full blast of this painful humiliation and disillusionment . . . For us it is the question mark about the motives of Pretoria which is trying to trick us into an independence which smells of fraud. They aim to continue their 'baasskap', privilege and discrimination, while shattering for ever my people's dreams of a place in the sun for all . . . It is perfectly true that the White Government has the power to do whatever they like with us. We are negotiating, at this moment; from a position of such complete powerlessness that they can do as they please. To anyone on the receiving end, it is not difficult to understand why some people feel tempted to resort to violence and terrorism for the sake of freedom."

Steve Biko, 31, Black Consciousness leader, is detained on 18 August in Grahamstown. He dies in detention on 12 September. His death is widely mourned in South Africa and draws condemnation from within and outside the country.

Desmond Tutu states: "God called Steve Biko to be his servant in South Africa—to speak up on behalf of God, declaring what the will of God must be in a situation such as ours, a situation of evil, injustice, oppression and exploitation. Through Steve, God sought to awaken in the Black person a sense of his intrinsic value and worth as a child of God, not needing to apologise for his existential condition as a Black person, calling on Blacks to glorify and praise God that He had created them black. Steve, with his brilliant mind that always saw to the heart of things, realised that until Blacks asserted their humanity and their personhood, there was not a remote chance for reconciliation in South Africa. For true reconciliation is a deeply personal matter. It can happen only between persons who assert their own personhood and who acknowledge and respect that of others. You don't get reconciled to your dog, do you? Steve knew and believed fervently that being pro-Black was not the same thing as being anti-White. The Black Consciousness Movement is not a 'hate White movement' despite all you may have heard to the contrary . . ."

Ten Black Consciousness organizations send an open letter to Chief Lucas Mangope, calling on him to stop assisting Pretoria in apartheid policy, and accusing him of playing an opportunist game, the consequences of which he would eventually have to face.

The Swazi Homeland enters the first stage of self-government when a Legislative Assembly is established. With the exception of Ndebele groups, all other Homelands have self-governing status.

Chief Kaizer Matanzima states that unless certain lands are returned to the Transkei, settlement of the dispute will only be attained by means of an armed struggle. He also threatens to annex the Ciskei, thus uniting all Xhosas into one nation.

On 6 December 1977 Bophuthatswana gains independence from the Republic of South Africa. Last night Chief Lucas Mangope in Mmabatho said: "In the same way that our self-respect prevents us from contemplating discrimination or revenge against our White fellow South Africans, our self-respect also makes it impossible to deny our well-founded bitterness on the issue of land in South Africa."

The Mohapi people in order to be accommodated and remain in parts of Bophuthatswana are forced to become Batswana, no longer Basotho; forced to become Barolong, no longer Bataung; forced to become Mogapi, no longer Mohapi because Bophuthatswana was meant for the Batswana only. In school there was no Sesotho language but Setswana.

The Modderdam settlement near Cape Town is demolished.

The number of Black people arrested in South Africa for pass law offences in 1977, far exceeds 200 000.

1978 In keeping with the South African Government's policy that there are no Black South Africans, acts are passed which erode the rights of Blacks to permanence in South Africa. They are declared foreigners and reduced to the status of foreigners in South Africa.

Black people are harassed on their 'illegal' settlements and their dwellings are destroyed and they are dumped in arid areas of the Homelands. The Whites have made the land too hot for the Black people to stay on.

1978 At a conference in Grahamstown on "South Africa: The Road Ahead", Chief Gatsha Buthelezi states that there are only two alternatives facing South Africa—an escalation of violence which will become chaotic and unmanageable, and negotiation.

The South African Black Alliance is established under the leadership of Chief Buthelezi. The main aim of the Alliance is to advance the struggle against apartheid.

The Azanian People's Organisation (AZAPO) is established to fill the leadership gap after the wholesale detention of Black leaders in October 1977. The main aim of AZAPO is to advance the struggle against apartheid. Subsequently the entire executive and some members of the local branches are detained.

Chief Gatsha Buthelezi is re-elected Chief Minister of Kwazulu Government.

Inkatha maintains its total rejection of independence for Kwazulu and of apartheid in South Africa.

Inkatha continues to call for the release of political prisoners and the holding of national convention to decide on a new political dispensation for South Africa.

Three freedom fighters are shot by the police after throwing a hand-grenade at a police patrol in Bophuthatswana. In another incident gunfire is exchanged between guerrillas and the Bop. Police and SA Police.

1978 A secret Government report on the mining industry, drawn up to enquire into the causes of riots on the mines, states, among other things, that the migratory system *per se* is at the root of the problem. According to the report, 33 of the 54 riots examined arose out of ethnic differences, and nearly all these clashes involved Xhosas and Basotho workers. It states that compound-life and the migrant system reinforced tribal differences.

A meeting of the chief ministers of all non-independent Homelands takes place and they all reject the policy of creating independent Homeland Republics in the Republic of SA.

President Lucas Mangope states in the first session of the first National Assembly of Bophuthatswana that any person, irrespective of race, can become the citizen of Bophuthatswana. He also signs a proclamation repealing the Mixed Marriages Act of 1949 and Section 16 of the Immorality Act of 1957.

Chief Tidimane Pilane, the leader of the opposition National Seoposengwe Party in Bophuthatswana states that the Homelands which have opted for independence have sold the birthright of their people.

1978 The Unibell 'illegal' settlement near Cape Town is demolished and about 20 000 Black people are left homeless. This treatment of Blacks strains the relations of the Republic of Transkei and the Republic of South Africa. The Republic of Transkei is thinking of breaking off diplomatic relations with the Republic of South Africa.

The Deputy Minister of Plural Relations (Blacks are regarded Plurals, not people), W.L. Vosloo warns: "Crossroads will be treated exactly the same way as Unibell."

30 June is declared a world day of prayer for the fate of the 'illegal' settlements in South Africa, specifically those in Crossroads on the Cape Flats. A petition is circulated which reads: "We, the people of Crossroads,

appeal to the authorities not to demolish Crossroads and appeal to the wider community to support us in our struggle to maintain family life."

Chief Kaizer Matanzima declares his intention of passing a legislation which will enable him to ban the Methodist Church of SA in Transkei. He is reacting to a report in the Methodist Church newspaper, "Dimension", which stated that a decision had been taken at the church conference in 1977 that the State President of SA would no longer receive messages of goodwill from the church, as this would necessitate sending similar message to the State President of Transkei and this would go against the views of Methodist clergy, who were opposed to and not recognize the independence of Transkei.

The Transkei Parliament passes the Undesired Organisations Act. It is evident that the Act, which was hurriedly passed through parliament, is in fact introduced in order to enable President Matanzima to take action against the Methodist Church of SA.

1978 Trouble flares up in the Thaba 'Nchu area when large numbers of Basotho are arrested by the Bophuthatswana police on charges of 'illegal' settlement. One person is shot.

In 1978, in his closing speech in the National Assembly, President Mangope stated: " . . . If one thing might cause war in South Africa, it will be land and its allocation".

President Mangope states that his country will not harbor people working to undermine South Africa.

During a no-confidence debate in the Transkei National Assembly, C. Diko, leader of the opposition Transkei People's Freedom Party, says that if Transkei wants international recognition it should dissociate itself from SA. He also reminds President Matanzima of his threat to declare war on South Africa if East Griqualand is not ceded to Transkei and urges him to carry out his threat.

South Africa's Parliament passes the Alteration of Provincial Boundaries Act which provides for the transfer of East Griqualand from the Cape Province to Natal Province. President Chief Matanzima announces in the Transkei

National Assembly that he is breaking off diplomatic ties with South Africa as a result of its refusal to hand over East Griqualand to Transkei. He also announces his decision to break the non-aggression pact between the two countries, Transkei and South Africa.

1978 Chief Lennox Sebe is re-elected Chief Minister of the Ciskei Homeland. He states that a one-party state has been created in Ciskei by the will of people.

Chief Sebe states that he will not opt for independence until Ciskei is economically independent and all her rightful land regained, from Fish River to the Kei River and from the Indian ocean to the Stormberg.

Prof. Hudson Ntsanwisi, Chief Minister of Gazankulu, also states that he will not opt for independence until such a time Gazankulu is economically independent.

Dr Cedric Phatudi of Lebowa strongly criticises Bophuthatswana and Transkei for having opted for independence. According to him the important issues are land distribution, economic viability and job creation.

1978 Robert Sobukwe pass on. He was an intellectual, Sobukwe was true to his conviction that a leader should not ask the people to do anything he would not do himself. His idea was that Africans would stop carrying passes, present themselves for mass arrest, fill the jails, and thus withdraw their labour to the system until the pass laws were abolished. Stop carrying them not merely as a gesture but as the beginning of the end of apartheid. That, he promised, would be a first step to an early triumph for Black nationalism.

1978 It is suggested in the Economic Review for QwaQwa that it should be developed a city-state for the Basotho, based on the lack of natural resources and severe overpopulation and no land extensions. Further resettlement of Basotho in QwaQwa should also be stopped.

Venda becomes the third Homeland to opt for independence. The Prime Minister announces that Venda will become independent during the latter half of 1979.

The Bophuthatswana government establishes a committee to examine rural and regional development, as well as an agricultural development corporation whose functions include the identification of possible development projects and their planning and implementation.

1979 P.W. Botha is the new Prime Minister of South Africa. He announces that he establishes a commission of enquiry to look into the land question comprising of academic leaders, Government leaders, economic leaders and Black leaders. No Africans are, however, represented on the committee.

Chief George Matanzima is the new Prime Minister of Transkei. Together with Chief Mangope, they reject recommendations made by the land commission. Mafikeng remains the only town to be annexed into Bophuthatswana. Recommendations meant massive resettlement of thousands of families from as far as Thaba 'Nchu, into one block of land called Bophuthatswana, around Mafikeng area.

Delegates at the Coloured Labour Party's annual conference, the theme of which is "A New South Africa" state that they see themselves as Blacks and do not want to be called "Coloured" or "Brown". David Curry, national chairman, states that the Coloured people will only be free when the African is free.

The Natal Indian Congress annual conference wants universal suffrage without special concessions to minority groups, a national convention, the repeal of discriminatory laws, the release of political prisoners and the return of exiles.

1979 Political disagreement between Chief Gatsha Buthelezi and members of the Soweto Committee of Ten erupts. Dr Nthato Motlana, Chairman of the Committee, states that there is no hope of establishing common ground with Chief Buthelezi, as he is involved in implementing government policy. Inkatha decides to contest the community council elections in Soweto.

Two Black student organisations are formed: The Congress of South African Students and the Azanian Students' Organisation.

Inkatha distributes pamphlets urging Blacks not to sell their South African birthright by taking out the Homelands' citizenship. The pamphlet is banned.

On 13 September Venda becomes the third Homeland to be granted independence by the South African Government. Chief Mphephu is declared the Paramount Chief of Venda.

Hendrik Coetzer states in the South African Assembly: "Inside and around Ciskei there is unemployment and hunger as nowhere else in South Africa".

Allegations of corruption are leveled against Transkeian government officials after disclosures by the Transkeian Minister of Finance. The unauthorized expenditure totaled R4, 7m.

1980 Inkatha accuses the Commission of Inquiry on the Constitution of RSA as being unrepresentative of South Africa's population and calls for national convention to discuss the constitution. Certain non-negotiable are enumerated: 1. One unitary state for South Africa and one nationality, one passport, one citizenship, one economy, one defence force, and one communications system. 2. Blacks to be included in the process of making and administering law and to share power within one political system. 3. Discriminatory laws must be repealed as a first step. 4. Blacks will consider proposals which would effectively consolidate existing Homelands and locate them as provinces in a political system which makes provision for regional responsibility. 5. Whites must accept that minority interests cannot continue to be protected by total White monopoly of power in politics and the economy (land and its wealth). The final protection of minority rights lies in the protection of individual rights.

The Schlebusch Commission recommends, *inter alia*, the appointment of a President's Council consisting of 60 members of the White, Coloured, Asian, and Chinese communities. Its function would be to advice the State President on any matter which in its opinion is of national interest. Blacks overwhelmingly reject the recommendations because of their exclusion from the President's Council and the proposal to establish a separate Black council.

1980 P.W. Botha meets the Homeland leaders who inform him that they stand by their statement of no-negotiable principles and propose a federal type of constitution. After the meeting Botha announces that the Government will not proceed with the establishment of an advisory, non-elective council for Africans. The five non-negotiable principles are: 1. Preference of unitary state as a first option. 2. Non-negotiable rejection of independent Homelands. 3. Non-negotiable rejection and dismissal of the 1913 and 1936 Land Acts as the basis for the division of land between Whites and Blacks. 4. Abolition of statutory race discrimination. 5. Retention of South African nationality and the right to South African passport.

At a public meeting in Soweto, Chief Gatsha Buthelezi urges Blacks to adopt a multi-faceted strategy to bring concerted political pressure to bear on the authorities, forcing them to hold a national convention. He states that the conditions for armed struggle are non-existent in South Africa.

1980 In an address to the European Parliament, Chief Buthelezi demands international recognition for Inkatha and states that international support for the military wing of the ANC will not help to bring about meaningful liberation for Blacks in South Africa. The ANC, he says, is not a government in exile and cannot claim to be representative of the Black people in South Africa. The South African struggle will be won by political means by those inside the country.

AZAPO condemns the Homelands policy as depriving Africans of South African citizenship, destroying Black unity and facilitating continued economic exploitation of Blacks. AZAPO envisages a state in which all persons will have right to ownership of property, including land and its wealth, and complete participation in the political machinery of the country. AZAPO defines Blacks as the oppressed people of the country and states that it is only the Black working class which has nothing to lose in a radical overthrow of the present system.

The Commission of Enquiry into the independence for the Ciskei finds that the majority of Ciskeians do not favour independence for Ciskei. It also finds that there is high level of infant mortality and a widespread of incidence of malnutrition in Ciskei; a serious housing shortage; there is also a severe overcrowding in the area. Land shortage is also found to be a problem. The Commission recommends that Ciskei should not opt for independence unless certain conditions are met. Commenting on the Commission's report, Chief Lennox Sebe tells the territory's legislative assembly that his administration will not follow its recommendation slavishly. Later in the year it becomes clear to the observers that Chief Sebe has nevertheless decided to opt for independence for the Ciskei.

The Government appears to concede that the Homelands policy is economic failure suffered by Blacks and that it will not be possible to relocate all urban Africans in the Homelands. The permanence of an urban African population is recognized. Nevertheless substantial relocation of Africans continues.

1980 Chief Lennox Sebe states that urban Blacks refusing to take out Homelands citizenships rob the Homelands, since South African Government grants are based on the population figures of the Homelands.

Dr Robert Rotberg of the Commission, states that the Homelands are too small, impoverished and developmentally unpromising to provide meaningful resources for the country's African population.

Prof. Christof Hannekom states that the idea that the social, economic and political development of urban Africans could be accommodated in the Homelands, is "a dangerous escape from reality" and that people who make such statements are living in "a fool's paradise, covered in ideological dust".

1980 Violence breaks out in the Matlala area of Lebowa following the refusal of the "Congress of the People" to accept the authority of the Lebowa administration. Resistance to apartheid Government by the people of Lebowa dates back to the passage of the hated 1913 Land Act, since which they have refused to move into defined residential areas, pay tax, accept regulations of controlling livestock or the amount of land they are allowed to plough. Mobs of Lebowa government supporters attack the people, killing two and injuring eighty others.

President Lucas Mangope announces that he favours White farmers retaining their land after incorporation into Bophuthatswana.

Batswana chiefs criticises Sun City that it lures Batswana girls into prostitution, drink and easy money. They say that the traditional values are being abandoned and that the "morals of our people" are "going to the dogs".

On 1 September 1980, Mafeking is incorporated into Bophuthatswana. The town's name is changed to the "original" Mafikeng. Remember that three months ago in 2011 the town's name was again changed to the "original" Mahikeng. And so what is its original name.

A state of emergency is declared in Transkei. It is aimed at preventing further unrest, following demonstrations at the University of Transkei. Corruption is reported to be rife in Transkei. Transkei announces that it is resuming diplomatic relations with South Africa.

The total number of Africans arrested by the police and administration board officials was 117 518.

1981 The National Party's election manifesto rejects the principle of one-man-one-vote in a one unitary state.

The question of citizenship is all important in the trial of Anthony Bobby Isotsobe. He is a freedom fighter convicted of treason in the Supreme Court of South Africa, Pretoria, and is sentenced to death. It is maintained, in his defence, that he is a citizen of Transkei and therefore does not owe allegiance (loyalty) to South Africa, but the argument is not accepted by the judge, Mr Justice Theron. Prof. Johan van der Vyfer states: "The judgement can be interpreted as making mockery of the independence of Homelands." Prof. John Dugard states that the judgement conflicts with the Government policy. Using the case of Nyanga squatters to illustrate the contradiction, Prof Dugard says: "It is impossible to deport people from Nyanga one day on the grounds that they are aliens (foreigners), and then to sentence those to death the next day on the ground that they owe allegiance to the State that declared them aliens."

1981 African political groups join some 55 other organisations in a countrywide campaign to boycott the 20th anniversary celebrations of the South African Republic.

Accusations that Inkatha is collaborating with the South African Government in the implementation of Apartheid policies become more vehement. Chairman of the Black Student Society at Wits University, D. Johnson, tells a gathering of 1 500 people that Chief Gatsha Buthelezi,

Inkatha leader, is a "Government lackey" who will be destroyed with other supporters of Apartheid system.

AZAPO continues to reject the SA Black Alliance under Chief Buthelezi's leadership as an organisation which is collaborating with Apartheid authorities. Delegates at AZAPO conference agree that the struggle for the re-possession of African land is central to their political programme.

1981 President Lucas Mangope does not recognise trade unions.

Ciskei becomes the fourth Homeland to gain independence from South Africa. Chief Lennox Sebe announces an independence "package deal" concluded with South African Government. He says that it will ensure that their independence is different from other independent Homelands. Among other things, it will enable Ciskeians to retain their identity while at the same time not surrendering their citizenship in South Africa. Chief Sebe's claims prove to be very hollow. The Secretary of Enquiry into the Independence for Ciskei Commission says that Chief Lennox Sebe was "hell bent" on independence, whatever the cost to the people.

The Government continues with its policy of forced removal of Blacks from land. one such case is the mass removal from St Wendolins, 12 km outside Pinetown. It is reported that 1 100 families are moved to two Kwazulu areas, KwaDabeka and KwaNdengezi. Among those still to be removed are 75 families with freehold title. In another case it is revealed that since August 1980, hundreds of homes had been demolished in Umbulwane, an African freehold area near Ladysmith. Controversy also arises over the planned removal of people from the Mbila tribe from the Sordwana Bay area (Natal) to allow for the further development of the Sordwana Bay holiday resort for Whites. Its people have been moved at least twice in past few years. In the OFS controversy arises over a report in the American Christian Science Monitor on the resettlement area of Onverwacht. The journal states that thousand of Africans are housed in iron shacks and live on 45 ft by 90 ft plots which are too small even for subsistence farming. It also disputes the official number of 65 000 residents, placing the number at 130 000. 25 000 Africans in the Ciskei are facing their fourth move since the 1960s. First move was when they were evicted from White farms and urban townships in the "Coloured labour preference" area of the Eastern Cape. They were then sent to resettlement camp called

Ilinge near Queenstown, but when this was ceded to the Transkei in 1976 they chose to move to another resettlement camp at Sada in the Ciskei, to avoid becoming Transkeian citizens. The Sada camp became grossly over-crowded and spawned its own sprawling squatter slum, the "Village of Tears", where even the basic facilities such as toilets do not exist. Much of the Sada overflow moved to Oxton—where there is no grazing land, no water, and the ground is so hard and stony to scratch out vegetable gardens. Now these families are yet to be moved, to Poplar Grove, between Sada and the small town of Whittlesea.

On 16 July 1981, about 1 500 people are arrested in a pre-dawn raid at Nyanga township outside Cape Town. They are people who have built rough shelters in the bush surrounding the township after their eviction from hostels in Langa. Several other raids follow, despite severe criticism from various organisations. A delegation of US congressmen are refused entry to the area, they condemn the "official inhumanity and brutality" of the Apartheid authorities.

1982 The President's Council advices the President that a united South Africa with one-man-one-vote is not a viable option. The Council is also against the democratic principle of majority rule. The Constitutional Committee rejects the idea of the bill of rights and instead recommends the inclusion of "a limited number of guarantees". Its President states: "The future of democracy is at stake if Africans are included in the constitutional plans for a new South Africa".

Inkatha rejects the President's Council report and states that "power sharing by forming an extended laager of Whites, Indians and Coloureds to the total exclusion of the Black masses will only lead to a political *cul-de-sac*".

1982 Khehla Mthebu of AZAPO states that he rejects racism in all its forms. However, the realistic situation in South Africa is that the oppressor is White as well as capitalistic. Thus, for the Blacks to win the struggle, they must become a strong one solid unit. According to him the President's Council has ignored the following very important points: (1). South Africa is the legitimate property of the Blacks. (2). Protection of individual and group freedom, protection of identity are "euphemisms for racist policies and principles which serve White interests and needs". (3). Equality of opportunity and justice, either in the present system, or the new South Africa envisaged is a myth.

Deputy Minister of Development admits that Black locations and townships were developed because they believed that the African was a foreigner and was here in South Africa temporarily; that he will return 'to his country he has never been or seen'.

P.W. Botha states that racial segregation of amenities, including beaches, residential areas and schools, will remain Government policy.

In his independence celebration speech President Lucas Mangope states that the money Bophuthatswana received in 1982 from South Africa represented only six percent of his country's budget of R500m.

Sheena Duncan of the Black Sash reveals that by 1981 almost 9 million Africans had lost their South African citizenship through the Government's Homelands Policy. These African effectively became 'foreigners' in their motherland, South Africa. Because of the status of being 'foreigners' Africans have lost their right to political participation and right to a fair share of the country's economic wealth.

Dr Nthato Motlana, chairman of the Soweto Committee of Ten, is refused a South African passport to attend a Conference in the United States. He is told by the Government to apply for a Bophuthatswana passport, but he refuses to do so. Please take note that Bophuthatswana passport mostly allowed Africans to travel to South Africa only.

The Government announces its plan that the KaNgwane Homeland and the Ingwavuma region of Kwazulu are to be handed over to Swaziland. Both the KaNgwane and Kwazulu governments reject the plan. Dr Peter Vale of the South African Institute of International Affairs claims that the land deal is a new way of "ditching" large numbers of Africans. Swaziland was to gain hundred thousands new citizens if the land deal was successful.

1982 Bophuthatswana's first general elections since independence are held in October. However, in Soweto only 135 people and in Ga-Rankuwa only 50 people vote. President Mangope's ruling party wins all the eight contested constituencies.

The Bophuthatswana government amends its Constitution Act, abolishing seats in the Legislative Assembly for nominated Chiefs. This makes Bophuthatswana the only Homeland in which elected members outnumber nominated Chiefs in the Legislative Assembly.

A group of students at the University of Fort Hare stones a motorcade in which President Lennox Sebe is being driven to the university's graduation ceremony. Two students are injured when Ciskei police open fire on them, and 1 500 are arrested.

Regarding Venda it is reported that Paramount Chief Patrick Mphephu's salary has increased by 121% in less than two years. After the increases, the Minister of Agriculture announces cutbacks in agricultural projects because there is no money.

Chief Gatsha Buthelezi repeatedly states that although Inkatha stands for one-person-one-vote in a unitary state, it is prepared to look at alternatives to find a peaceful solution. Black majority rule will probably lead to civil war. The Chief states that a consociational form of government with a vote for all the races, and checks and balances to protect minority groups, will be the best way of pooling skills and human resources.

In an article published by the Development Studies Group, Marion Lacey states that between 1960 and 1980, only 75 000 jobs had been created within all the Homelands through development corporation investment. A further 75 000 jobs had been created in border industries over the same period. Lacey states that in 1976 the development corporations invested R42m for the Blacks in Homelands, which was only 2% of the total money invested for the Whites in 'White South Africa'.

1982 The Government continues with its policy of forced removals, with no indication that it intends changing it.

The South African Defence Force launched a raid on ANC offices in Maputo, Mozambique, killing thirteen people.

In August 1982 the activist Ruth First was opening her post in Maputu, where she was living in exile, when she was murdered by a letter bomb. She was the wife of Joe Slovo. Her death revealed the extent of the state's cruelty in combating the struggle for freedom.

In December 1982, Umkhondo we Sizwe (MK) set off explosions at the unfinished Koeberg nuclear power plant outside Cape Town and placed bombs at many other military and apartheid targets around the country.

The same month, the South African military attacked an ANC outpost in Maseru, Lesotho, killing forty-two innocent men, women and children.

In May 1983 the MK struck at an air force and military offices in the heart of Pretoria with its first car bomb attack. Nineteen people were killed and more than two hundred injured.

The armed struggle escalates. Oliver Tambo states: "The armed struggle was imposed upon us by the violence of the apartheid regime".

Apartheid army and police platoons and troops are deployed into Black locations and townships.

The United Democratic Front (UDF) is formed. The UDF blossomed into a powerful organisation that united over six hundred anti-apartheid organisations—trade unions, community groups, church groups, and student associations.

Bishop Desmond Tutu travels the world over calling for the nations across the globe to impose economic sanctions on the Government of South Africa. The government is under growing international pressure.

Nelson Mandela in prison states to Lord Bethell of the European Parliament: "It is not up to us to renounce violence, but the government. I reaffirm you that we aim for hard military objects, not people."

On 31 January 1985, P.W. Botha states: "I offer Mr. Mandela release from prison if he unconditionally rejects violence as a political instrument. It is therefore not the South African government which now stands in the way of Mr. Mandela's freedom but it is Mr. Mandela himself".

On Sunday 10 February 1985, Nelson Mandela's daughter Zindzi read his response to Botha to the cheering crowds who have not been able to hear his words for more than twenty years: " . . . What freedom am I being offered while the ANC remains banned? What freedom am I being offered when I may be arrested on a pass offence? What freedom am I being offered to live my life as a family with my dear wife who remains in banishment in Brandfort? What freedom am I being offered when I must ask for permission to live in town? . . . What freedom am I being offered when my very South African citizenship is not respected? . . . I cannot and will not give any undertaking at a time when I and you, the people, are not free. Your freedom and mine cannot be separated."

Mandela is separated from his prison mates and was taken to a new cell on the ground floor. He writes a letter to the Minister of Justice, Kobie Coetsee, pressing him for the meeting to discuss talks between the ANC and the government. The Minister chose to ignore the prisoner, not once, but several times.

The Eminent Persons Group, from the British Commonwealth, visits Mandela in May 1986. Mandela states to them: "I am not the head of the movement. The head of the movement is Oliver Tambo in Lusaka. You must go and see him. You can tell him what my views are, but they are my personal views alone. They don't even represent the views of my colleagues here in prison. All that being said, I favour the ANC beginning discussions with the government".

Nelson Mandela writes in his book 'Long Walk To Freedom': "After the group had finished with me, they planned to meet both Oliver Tambo in Lusaka and the government officials in Pretoria. In my remarks, I had sent messages to both places. I wanted the government to see that under the right circumstances we would talk, and I wanted Oliver to know that my position and his were the same".

President Botha responds by launching air raid and commando attacks on ANC bases in Botswana, Zambia and Zimbabwe. This utterly poisoned the talks, and the Eminent Persons Group immediately left South Africa. Once again Mandela's efforts to move negotiations forward had stalled.

The people are committed to render the country ungovernable. The state of political unrest and violence is reaching new heights. On 12 June 1986 the government imposed a State of Emergency in an attempt to stop political protests.

Mandela, at last, manages to meet with the Minister of Justice and request to meet P.W. Botha and Pik Botha because the time had come for negotiations, not fighting, and that the government and the ANC should sit down and talk.

Oliver Tambo holds a meeting with the US secretary of state, George Shultz.

The National Party has never been stronger. In the White general election of May 1987, the NP won an overwhelming majority.

1989 UDF forms an alliance with COSATU to form the Mass Democratic Movement, which then began organising a countrywide defiance campaign to challenge apartheid.

Oliver Tambo holds talks with the governments of Great Britain and the Soviet Union.

1989 Nelson Mandela holds talks with the government of South Africa; in the form of meeting President P.W. Botha for the very first time. He asked President Botha to release unconditionally all political prisoners including himself. President Botha turns down his request and a month later President Botha resigned as a state president. He accused his cabinet members of a breach of trust, of ignoring him and of playing into the hands of ANC.

F.W. De Klerk is sworn in as acting president and affirmed his commitment to change and reform. He states that his government is committed to peace and that it would negotiate with any other group committed to peace.

Bishop Tutu is leading a big protest march in Cape Town, the first unbanned march since the march led by Phillip Kgosana in 1960. De Klerk eases restrictions on political gatherings and marches which have been put in place since 1960.

On 15 October 1989 De Klerk released Mandela's former Robben Island comrades.

De Klerk began to dismantle many of the building blocks of apartheid. He opened South African beaches to people of all colours. He undertakes to stop segregating parks, theaters, restaurants, buses, libraries, toilets and other public facilities according to race. The National Security Management System, a secret service structure set up to combat anti-apartheid organisations, would also be dissolved.

In December 1989 Mandela writes a letter to De Klerk. Mandela writes: " . . . Your government had spent too much time talking with Black Homelands leaders and others co-opted by the system; these men are the agents of an oppressive past that the mass of Black South Africans reject . . . The current conflict is draining South Africa's lifeblood and talks are the only solution. The ANC would accept no preconditions to talks. The Harare Declaration of 1989 put the onus on the government to eliminate the obstacles to negotiations that the state itself had created. Those demands included the release of all political prisoners, the lifting of all bans on restricted organisations and persons, the ending of the State of Emergency and the removal of all troops from the townships. A mutually agreed-upon cease-fire to end hostilities ought to be the first order of business, for without that, no business could be conducted".

On 13 December 1989, Mandela and De Klerk meet for the first time in Tuynhuys. Mandela tells De Klerk that their five-year plan proposals are unacceptable to the ANC because the NP 'group rights' is a means of preserving White dominance. He tells De Klerk that it is like he wants to modernise apartheid without abandoning it." An oppressive system cannot be reformed", Mandela said;" it must be entirely cast aside. The ANC has not struggled against apartheid only to yield to a disguised form of it. We cannot allow for the bringing back of apartheid through the back door".

On 2 February 1990 F.W. De Klerk lifts the ban on political parties and thirty-one other illegal organisations and announces the freeing of political prisoners incarcerated for non-violent activities; the suspension of capital punishment; and the lifting of various restrictions imposed by the State of Emergency. He declared: "The time for negotiation has arrived".

On Sunday 11 February 1990 the world watched the release of Nelson Mandela after 27 years in prison.

1990 The ANC leaders and the Inkatha leader forgo the golden opportunity to meet each other and iron out differences in pursuit for unity and peace. Their relations deteriorated and finally it led to the ANC-IFP war; Black on Black Battle in Kwazulu-Natal and Gauteng. Thousands of Black people died horrific deaths.

Mandela states to a crowd of over 100 000 people at King's Park in Kwazulu-Natal: "Take your guns, your knives and your pangas, and throw them into the sea! End this war now!" The war and its atrocities continued.

26 March the apartheid police massacre people in Sebokeng, wounding hundreds and killing twelve ANC demonstrators. As a result 'talks about talks' are suspended by the ANC: 'Mr de Klerk cannot be allowed to talk about negotiations on the one hand and murder our people on the other'.

Talks about talks between the ANC and NP takes place in May 1990 over a period of three days. About this talks Mandela points out that the meeting represented an end to the master/servant relationship that characterized Black and White relations in South Africa.

The talks about talks brought about the signing of Groote Schuur Minute, pledging both sides to a peaceful process of negotiations and lifting of the State of Emergency.

The 'Black on Black Violence' escalates in the Vaal Triangle. The police, the defence force and the IFP are suspected to be working together to weaken the ANC and the liberation struggle, to destabilize the country and forestall negotiations for the birth of a new South Africa.

22 July 1990 busloads of armed Inkatha members, escorted by apartheid police entered Sebokeng to attend a rally. After the rally the armed men went on rampage, murdering approximately thirty people in a dreadful and grisly attack. The apartheid police made not a single attempt to protect the people of Sebokeng.

6 August 1990 the ANC and NP signed the Pretoria Minute in which the ANC agreed to suspend the armed struggle.

In November 1990 a group of IFP members entered Zonkizizwe near Germiston, and attacked people, killing a number of people and drove the rest out from their homes and place. The IFP members occupy their abandoned homes and confiscate all the property. The surviving ex-residents of Zonkizizwe still claim that the IFP members were accompanied by the police. In the wake of this tragedy, the police and the government made no arrests and took no action.

Concerning this tragedy Mandela meets de Klerk and Adriaan Vlok, his minister of law and order. About Adriaan Vlok, Mandela writes: "His attitude was that of many Afrikaners who believe that Black tribes had been killing each other since time immemorial".

Nelson Mandela writes: "During this time, the government took another action that added fuel to the flames. It introduced a regulation permitting Zulus to carry so-called 'traditional weapons' to political rallies and meetings. These weapons, assegais, which are spears, and knobkerries, wooden sticks with heavy wooden head, are actual weapons with which Inkatha members killed ANC members. This gave me grave doubts about Mr. De Klerk's peaceful intentions."

The South African newspaper reports disclose that the South African police had secretly funded Inkatha.

In December 1990 Oliver Tambo returned to South Africa, having been in exile from his motherland for thirty years.

Each day the newspapers were filled with fresh reports of 'Black on Black Violence'. In March 1991 Alexandra is attacked by the Inkatha, forty-five people were killed and again no one was arrested.

Mandela travelled twice to meet Buthelezi in Kwazulu-Natal as an effort to bring peace between the ANC and the IFP, but his efforts were a failure. And the violence continued.

May 1991 the ANC suspends talks with the government and begin to have second thoughts about the suspension of armed struggle.

September 1991 the ANC and the government signs a National Peace Accord.

On 20 December 1991, after two years of 'talks about talks', the real talks began: CODESA—Convention for a Democratic South Africa. All South African political parties were to be in attendance. The PAC boycotted the talks, accusing the ANC of conspiring with the NP to form a multi-racial government. Chief Buthelezi also boycotted the talks on the ground that he was not permitted three delegations: for Inkatha, the KwaZulu government and King Zwelithini. The ANC argued that the King should be above politics, and that if he were included then every tribe should be allowed to send their paramount chiefs.

On the night of 17 June 1992, a heavily armed force of Inkatha members ambushed Boipatong township and killed forty-six people. It was the fourth massacre of ANC people that week. No arrests and no government investigations into the slaughtering of people.

ANC suspends talks and direct dealings with the apartheid government.

People were angry and frustrated; they made a call to Mandela to give them weapons. Some of the signs in rallies read, 'MANDELA, GIVE US GUNS' and 'VICTORY THROUGH WAR NOT WORDS'.

4 August 1992 one hundred thousand people march to the Union Buildings in Pretoria. They are addressed by Mandela.

7 September 1992 seventy thousand people march to Bisho in Ciskei. The police of this Bantustan led by Brigadier General Oupa Gqozo, open fire on the marchers and killed twenty-nine people, wounding over two hundred.

On 26 September 1992 Mandela and de Klerk signed the Record of Understanding for negotiations to continue.

On 10 April 1993 Chris Hani, the secretary-general of the SACP, the former chief of staff of MK and one of the most popular figures in the ANC, is assassinated in front of his home in Boksburg, Johannesburg.

The same day Mandela addressed the nation: "Tonight I am reaching out to every single South African, black and white, from the very depths of my being. A white man, full of prejudice and hate, came to our country and committed a deed so foul that our whole nation now teeters on the brink of disaster . . ." Mandela, with God given wisdom and skill, managed to halt the country from descending into civil war.

On 3 June 1993, after months of negotiations, the multi-party forum voted to set a date for the country's first national, non-racial, one-person-one-vote election: 27 April 1994.

On 27 April 1994 all South Africans, both Black and White, voted for the very first time in the history of South Africa. More than any one else, Black people were in high spirits. They thought that that was the breaking of chains of poverty, deprivation, and suffering.

On 10 May 1994 Nelson Rolihlahla Mandela was inaugurated to become the first Democratic President of the Republic of South Africa. The very first Black man to lead the political dispensation of South Africa.

THE LIFE OF BLACK PEOPLE AFTER 1994

After 1994 the owner of the land came on to the land. He came in a land rover. The man watched uneasily when the land rover drove along the fields. And at last the owner of the land drove into the door yard and sat in his car to talk to the man. The man stood beside the land rover for a while and listened. When he opened his mouth to plead, the land rover was gone and he was in a thick cloud of dust. Avoiding facing his wife and children with tears in his eyes, the man sat on his heels and found a stick with which to scrap the land.

In the open door way the woman stood looking out, and behind her stood beautiful children. The woman and the children watched the father and the owner of the land talk. They watched the owner of the land refusing to listen to their hope. They watched the owner of the land covering their father with a thick cloud of dust. A thick cloud of silence and unhappiness settled on the man's house. Children could not play and there was no humming from the mother in the kitchen preparing food.

In the dark of night the father talks to the mother. "Dear woman, the mother of my children, *die klein baas se ons moet gaan. Ek vra waar na toe. Hy se gaan, gaan, gaan!*"

The father turns slowly from facing the wall, not to face the mother but to face the roof.

The mother keeps dead silent in order to conceal her silent cry in the dark. She knows that she must be strong for the man and children. She must not show any weakness to them or their whole world shall comes tumbling down.

After a long silence and slowly as if counting the words, the father says to the mother: "The owner of the land says that he is not his own father. He says that I was allowed to live here by his father. He says he is the new owner of the land. He says that he has never given me permission to live here and he wants nobody to live in his land, *finish en klaar.*"

"Remember dear mother he started forcefully removing those who had less than twenty years on the land. By then I never thought that he shall count up to more than sixty. Today he got me and I am the last one. I am sixty years old on this land. I was born on this land. My father was born on this land. My grandfather and father are buried on this farm.

When I was a little boy my grandfather used to tell me that the whites found his grandfather already living on this land of rolling hills and valleys. One other day the whites divided the land among themselves. They have receipts and papers and court stamps as proof that they have purchased the land. But grandfather maintained up to the day he died that the whites have bought the land that was never sold. Our land was never sold. It was kind of a smash and grab crime. What an injustice!

By God and by my ancestors I swear that I am the owner of this land although it is illegal to say that in the courts of South Africa. They have made injustice legal. I am not going anywhere."

His wife cautioned: "The father of my children you have done all what a strong brave man like you could do. You have resisted this injustice for too long. In the course of resistance you lost all that was rightly yours—the spring water is poisoned; the results are your cattle are dead; your goats and sheep gone; pigs and chicken gone and the last piece of land you cultivated for years is taken by the owner of the land. He got papers that say it too belongs to him. Father of my children, *motaung ea motle, hle,* you must now bend or you shall break. And I still love you and the children need you. Let us go to where others have gone; God shall provide. Let's go and start again. God shall provide. (*A little silence*) Face this side *moratuoa,* come closer and take a rest my dear strong one"

Instead of taking a rest, he kissed her and on top he could not perform. The mother tried to arouse him to the game of love and play. She gave up disappointed after finding him ice cold. He raged and cried in her arms. "Is a man a man no more because of this injustice?" he sobs. Not silent sobs but a little loud baby's cry.

He tried to sleep but he could not fall asleep. After sometime he turned and faced the wall. Again he tried to sleep but he could not fall asleep. The clock in the living room ticking loudly like never before. After another sometime he turned and faced the roof. He begins to think that the clock is irritating. He blames it on the clock for not falling asleep, but it is very undesirable for him to get out of bed and disconnect the clock. He tells himself that he shall bear it for tonight and early in the morning disconnect the cell and throw it to 'that place you know'.

A long while later he jumped from the bed and knelt down and prayed: "Our forefathers who died many years ago and who toiled this land before us. Our ancestors whose good will and high merit deeds to the people and creation are not recorded and thus not commended. Our beloved departed parents who taught us to love and not to hate. Our parents we loved; our parents we still love and our parents we will forever love. Dear parents who used to comfort us when we cried. Can't you see our tears? Can't you see we are crying? Can't you see that we are suffering? The last piece of land we rightfully inherited from you is taken from us by the strong and powerful. We are helpless. Please intercede on our behalf and ask God the Creator and Almighty to help. You told us that God created us with the soil from the ground of this land. That makes us one with this land. It gives us right by birth to belong. By birth we belong to this land and the land belongs to us. We with the land are one. And the land with us is one. Forced separation is indistinguishable to death. They make us less than what God the Creator intended us to be. God created us to love this land and His creation; to work this land; and to play and be happy on this land. Oh Lord God, please open the eyes of the owners of the stolen land before it is too late. Awaken their conscience. Make them realise that we too are people created in Your image. Please make them aware that we, also as people, need a piece of land to call our own. We have seen it with our eyes; we know it, that a people without a land are nothing but a lesser people. That is why we are still today lesser than them the owners of the captured land. We pray Oh Lord that one day we will wake up to find the land in South

Africa belonging to South Africa and its entire people. But you know that we have waited too long. How long should we wait? Please dear God help us to bring into effect the Freedom Charter written by our forefathers and foremothers. Then they wrote that the land belong to all who live in it. Our forefathers and foremothers your toil and shed blood can not be in vain. We do not ask that they should be forcefully removed from land—as they did to us. We do not want another Zimbabwe, please Lord. We are only asking for a share of land and its wealth. Let them remain with the bigger share. The little share they give us shall make a big difference on our individual lives. Or are we asking too much God? Little land ownership will make us more human—better people. The Word of God says that God created human beings to have power and control over the fish, the birds, and all animals, wild and domestic and to have control over land and on land. In the squatter camp there are no animals, no birds, no fish and no land. There in the squatter camp four to five hundred families share less than one square kilometer. There I am not allowed to keep cattle or sheep or goat or pig or chicken. How can I take charge of these animals as Your Word says I should; whereas I am put into a system that shall eventually make me loose charge over myself and control over my children? Lord look I am trembling. I am afraid. I cry and shake like a little child Lord. Please Lord I am afraid. I am not going. Please Lord. Let it be. Amen."

The mother says a prayer: "God Almighty we thank you. We thank you for the love that you continue to reveal to us. We know because of your love we are not in the worst of worst situation. We thank you for the air we breathe and the healthy lungs that pump this air in our chests. We thank you for the flowers that blossoms and we thank you for the eyes to see these beauty. We thank you for the birds that sing on the trees and we thank you for the ears to hear these melodies. We thank you for the rain and seasons that come and goes. We thank you for not going and remaining with us. We thank you for the sun and the moon and the stars that light up the skies at night and the eyes to see this beauty. Your creation is beautiful. Your creation is good. We thank you for the limbs and minds we use in advancement of your creation and so that your will should be done on earth as it is in heaven. We thank you for the creative minds that separate us from other uncreative animals and creatures. We thank you for saving our souls. We thank you for the mouths to say Your praises. Thank you Oh Lord. And please teach us to love, not to hate. Amen"

After praying the father sits on the bed. He is thinking deeply. After two hours or so he stands up straight and still. Looks up to heaven. He shakes his head sharply. Three fists to the head. Shaking of the head. He is confused. He can not think straight. He walks from corner to corner. The mother is shaking with fear of this strange behaviour. The father talks to himself and the mother can not make sense of what he is saying. In his talk there are lots of yes—yes and no—no. For the first time the mother can not comprehend her husband and friend of many years.

The mother gets up from bed. She gently put her warm gentle hand on his shoulder. The touch was soft and sweet. He felt the warmth and the tender touch of her naked body making luscious and delicious contact with his naked skin. And her smell was tantalizing and tempting. He came back from the clouds and instantly he was breathing through his mouth. The mother steals a look at him and finds him strong, handsome, and beautiful at the same time. She was tempted to touch him and he was a hot rod. The mother kisses him sweetly on the open lips and suppresses her feelings and gently pushes him away from her and turns him off by mentioning the great trek thing to the squatter camp. 'Anyhow it is morning and children are up', she said to conclude and seal the matter.

The mother quickly dresses up. Slowly the father put on his clothes and loudly cries: 'What is this?'

What is this?

Botha was a president
We had oppressive yoke
We had no rights
We had wrongs
And we had no land

De Klerk came
To help fighters and martyrs
Free freedom fighters
Free Mandela
Free you and me

Mandela became our president
Made a serious undertake
'Never, never and never again
Shall it be that this beautiful land experience
The oppression of one by the other
And suffer the indignity
Of being the skunk of the world'

Mbeki became our president
Motlanthe became our president
Zuma became our president and still
We are the poorest of the poor
The skunk of the world
And still we have no land
We have rights and wrongs
We have oppressive poverty
And thus we are not free
Yes, the sun can not wait
And my son can not wait
And the hope can not wait
For it is draining and wearing out
And the hunger can not wait
For it can not be postponed
And the lives of many are wasted
In stinking poverty and hunger
For a child can not sing
For a child can not smile
In birth rights water downed system
And so mama what is this?

Before the mother could answer, the owner of the land sends a truck driver to tell them that out of kindness he has decided to give them a bonus day on the land. Prepare for a new life tomorrow in a brand new squatter camp. Truth is he forgot that today is the auction day.

The father takes nothing and walks up to the hills; where the sun rises. Before he hurries out he says to the mother that it is only children who can start again; he can not start again. 'Only children can start again' he says it to himself and to the trees as he walks, over and over again.

The land was very important to the man. It made him. The land was part of him. He was part of it. He was one with the land. He was whole with the land. It was his family and his darling. Forced removal from land plunged a knife into his heart because a place where people live is that people. To remove a people from the land is to cut a people in two. People are not whole without the land. People are not alive any more.

The man looked at the empty houses of former neighbours, sad and lonely; looking like ghost houses. But once there was laughter and happiness in those houses; there were parties and dancing and weddings. There were births and deaths and parties and ceremonies in those houses. There were people and there was life and it was good and holy. But, sadly, the new South Africa came and the owner of the land came to drive away the people from land.

XXX XXX XXX

On the edges of towns and townships and locations, in fields and in vacant lots the squatter camps popped up like bubbles from the water. Maybe our people fought for this land too much and too long up to the point of having bubbles like water. Squatter camps and shanty towns and informal settlements and tents and enclosures made of plastics of many colours and boxes of different sizes and all kinds of rejected material bubbled up everywhere in the new South Africa except on the land of the owner of the land. They jumped up everywhere, on inhabitable land and on uninhabitable land; even on the banks of streams and rivers and inside dry streams and rivers and when the rain season come—only South Africa knows, no; only the skunks know because they are the only ones who experience this.

They are the ones who know how it feels to see your small child quivering in wet cold clothes and having no other dry clothes to put on because all clothes are soaking and wet.

They are the ones who know how it feels to sleep with your baby on a wet muddy mattress with wet muddy sheets.

They are the ones whose belongings are swept away by water.

They are the ones who know how it feels to stand the whole night on your feet with a small child crying in your arms because there is no place to sit on or sleep on.

They are the ones who know exactly how it feels for your child to cry out of thirst without water to drink inside the flooded house.

They are the ones who know how sickening it is to hate day and night, to hate summer and winter, to hate life and death, to hate rainy seasons and dry seasons, to hate all seasons and all times and all creatures and who created them.

They are the ones whose children are drowned by the flood water.

They are the ones who know how it smells and feels and maybe tastes to live in a flooded house with all kinds of waste and human excrement from the hip of rubbish next-door.

They are the ones, I think, who the great state man, Nelson Mandela, meant when he said never shall it be that people suffer the indignity of being the skunks of the world.

Apartheid was bad and evil. This democracy many see it as a failure in regard to eradicating the pain of poverty and suffering to the Black people. It fails to restore to the Black people their livelihood, self sufficiency, and self-reliance taken from them by apartheid.

People can not be free without money.

People can not be free without land to live on.

People are not free if they cannot choose to live where they like but to live in the extremely overpopulated squatter camps.

People are not be free if they can not build their own houses but wait for RDP houses.

People are not free if they can not buy their own food but wait for food parcels from government.

People are not free if they can not earn their own money but wait for a little grant from government. People are not free if they can not work, play and love but forced to be jobless, to hate, fear and suffer in poverty.

People are not free to choose to live or die, but to die. People are not free and are unhappy to be named dirty and lazy to work whereas there is no work.

People can not eat politics.

People can not live on politics and promises but on land. People can not build their houses on politics and promises but on land.

People are not free when they can not be happy.

People are unhappy, angry, confused and nearing the breaking point.

South Africa must bring change in our land before it is too late. Black people have hoped and suffered too long and too much.

I think the government of the new South Africa is like a small boy in the playground with a small piece of cake, crowded by all other boys fighting for a share from it; whilst the big bully boy sits contented on the other half and more of the play ground, with the whole big cake far bigger than he can chew or his tummy can take multiplied by hundreds times.

I think in the new South Africa I am like a monkey which was fastened on ground by a short chain to a very short pole and it became excited to see its owner lengthening the height of the pole and it forgot to demand the lengthening of the chain. So the length of the chain remained the same and, as before the lengthening of the pole, it still can not reach the refreshing shadows and sweet fruits of neighbouring trees. It is told that: "You have now gained your freedom. The pole is lengthened you can run up and down it, free like others." Then it was happy for freedom, but today, it sits down without playing and sadly looks and envies the privileged monkeys playing freely on tree tops.

XXX XXX XXX

As the man walked he surveyed the land, the fields, the soil, the grass, the trees, the hills and their small river that twisted between the hills. He took a long look at the hills and the trees, even at the birds; all kinds of birds; leisurely taking a drink from the pool. His long look at things was as if to memorise them for eternity.

He remembers how his grandmother loved to tell beautiful stories about the land and the river and the rain and the sun. The memory is so vivid and is almost as if he hears her voice telling it now. He remembers his childhood games and plays with other children.

He remembers as a child walking the fields with his grandfather; teaching him the names of birds and animals and trees and kinds of grass. He remembers his grandfather teaching him how to catch fish; birds and wild animals. He remembers his grandfather teaching him which wild fruits to eat and which fruits of the land not to eat. Fruits—both on ground and on trees.

He remembers walking in the graveyard with his father; teaching him the links of past four generations. He remembers his mother telling him that a real person is the one who keeps connected to his/her roots and passing on this connection to his/her children. He remembers that his father always concluded visits to the graves by telling him that a real man is a man who knows himself. 'Know thyself' he said.

He remembers that his first ever love making was after bathing and swimming in this very same pool and then vanishing into that tall grass dragging a girl in his hand; now the mother of his children. He remembers how she was refusing but willing. He remembers how she cried and giggled at the same time. He remembers how she looked and breasted and even smelled. The memory is very rich and lively. He even remembers where the exact spot of love making was in the tall grass. Surely still the spot is grassless because there was a lot of tearing, and shredding and ripping of the grass. And it was good, it was sweet . . . oh, it was holy. As he stands up and walks searching in the direction of the tall grass he thinks: 'Oh Lord my God, how sweet it was! How quick do our days go by? It all seems like yesterday'.

The man spends the whole day out in the land. He saved the grave yard for last. Towards sunset he said a long goodbye to the hills and the pool and the birds and the trees and the grass and the spot. He then turned and walked slowly towards the graveyard. He arrived at the graveyard. In his mind's eye the dead became alive with him and one with him. He felt their presence and warmth and talked to them and they talked to him. Temporarily he felt at home and at ease. He spends three hours with his forefathers and foremothers. And lastly he says a long goodbye to the graveyard. Deep down he knows that he shall never walk into this graveyard again. He knows that it is the last time he caresses the physical connection he has with his ancestors. He feels that now they have just died the second death and they are gone forever. He feels deeply lost and deeply pained.

He walks back home under the beautiful bright moonlight sky. But to him there is no beauty. There is no brightness only dimness almost dark. His heart is heavy and he feels every beat and he hears every loud beat. Suddenly there was no air to breath and it was difficult to breathe and walk at the same time. After twelve meters he nearly felt down. His powerlessness to walk forced him to cut a walking stick from the nearest tree. He dragged himself homewards. He had to take break after walking short distances.

The man arrived at home very late and very old and very spent—he looked hundred years old. He finds the mother and the children waiting for him to pray together as usual. Fear and loss settled in the hearts of the mother and children because their father was spent and sick. For the first time he could not lead them in the Lord's Prayer. The father could not eat instead he asked for homemade mageu and drank it. The mother tucked him to sleep.

Early the next morning, the owner of the land came with a truck; he took the father and the mother and the children and all their worldly possessions and dumped them in the squatter camp 37 kilometers away from the land. The owner of the land hurried back to the land of rolling hills and valleys and twisting rivers and springs and pools. The land is of abundance, plenty and beauty. South Africa is rich and beautiful—sadly only to a few.

XXX XXX XXX

In his book 'Hope and Suffering' the great father of the people; Desmond Tutu writes: "Once upon a time, people came from a far away country and they touched down in our land. They just wanted to stop a little while before setting off on their journey to their destination in the lands of the rising sun. After a while some of these people decided to live in our land. They drove away some of the native people they found. They built castles and cultivated the land which they have captured. They took the native people and caused them to work without much remuneration because in those far off days you could own another human being as you owned your cattle or your dog, or your wagon. And then another people who looked like the first and also came from away the seas but who spoke a different language also came to our land. They were much stronger than the first people and so they took charge of the country—our country (our land)."

Before you dismiss these words written nearly thirty years ago as racist, outdated, and irrelevant; please first take a deep thought and answer the following questions. Are our brothers and sisters still caused to work without much remuneration in many private entities and farms? Are our brothers and sisters still treated worse than owned dogs by driving with a dog in the front and them, in all kinds of weather, at the back of an open van? *Ao banna!* The land, is the land still captured? If you answer yes to any of the above questions it means that it is about time Desmond Tutu writes a book **'Hoped and Suffered too long'**. How about that great man of all times, Nelson Mandela, writing **'Longest walk to freedom'**?

XXX XXX XXX

And then in the squatter camp the mother and the father must start all over again. They were dumped towards sunset on top of other squatters because there was no open land. The family is unwelcome and people come and look at them with deep hatred and unpleasant remarks that worry them.

"Are these people mad by keeping on coming here?" a red eyed thug with scars on the face questions out loud for all to hear.

The thug continues with asking questions and threatening with big red eyes: "Can't you see that there is no living space here? Where do you come from? Do not unpack, take your belongings and go back to where you come from. You are not staying here and you are not sleeping here tonight or you shall know us after nine"

"They are old, where have they been all their years? Maybe they only came so as to get an RDP house," the other thug shoots.

"No it can't be. They will be long time dead before the water and RDP houses come," the sophisticated one said.

"If it is not for RDP house then tell me what it is for," the red eyed demanded.

Then the father felt that the cruelty is enough and as the head of the family came to the defense of the family. He opened his mouth to speak but the words stuck on his throat. He searched for words the words were lost. His mouth remained wide open. The father breaks down to tears and wept bitterly in front of his children and other children. *You know how cruel other children can be.* They laughed. His knees failed him and he fell to the ground. The mother came running from the hip of their belongings with a towel to cover him from the face of the cruel world. Women came running from standing on the doors of their dirty filthy stinking flea ridden skunk enclosures to help the mother; a stranger to them. Men also came to drive away the rogues.

The father lay sprawled on the ground. The father seemed to be struggling; all his muscles contracted. And suddenly he bumped on the ground as though under a heavy blow. He lay still and his breath was stopped. A woman gently took the mother to the far side of the tight circle of men and women. A man knelt down and parted the tight jaws apart and reached his fingers into the father's throat for the tongue. And as he lifted it clear, a clattering breath came out, and a moaning breath was drawn in. The man found the stick on the ground and used it to keep the tight jaws apart, and slowly the weeping breath came out and in.

The mother jumped like a headless chicken. 'Pray,' she said. 'Pray, people please pray'. The woman held her from charging into the crowd. 'Pray, I command you, pray!'

The man kneeling on the ground looked up at the mother for a moment. The rattling breath became louder and more roughly. Then he prayed: "*Modimo wa boikanyo, re ikanya mo go Wena. O gogile—*"

'Hallelujah—Amen' the mother cried.

"*Borraetsho mo dinageng tsa lenyora. Mme re lopa ka tlhoafalo masego a ba a boneng. O nne Modimo wa rona, Mothusi mo tshikatshikeng. Mo ditseleng tsa botshelo goga dikgato tsa rona; Re tle re fitlhe kwa O teng*".

'*Re tle re fitlhe kwa O teng*. Hallelujah—Amen. *Re tle re fitlhe kwa O teng*' said the mother.

The father's eyes found the mother's eyes; their eyes inter-locked. The father's eyes were clear and deep and penetrating, and there was a knowing tranquil in them. The mother sat down beside him and put his head on her lap and removed the stick from his mouth.

The father closed his eyes and took a long gasping breath. The mother closed her eyes and said: 'Go on praying, *moruti,* go on".

"*Re tle re-fitlhe-kwa-O teng. Legaeng je re le batlang. Re-*" And the man stopped praying.

All the noise and activities has stopped in the entire camp. Then a loud burst of a release of air. And breathing stopped and every one said: 'Amen'. The father lay still. Deep silence settled over the camp. The mother closed his eyes properly and kissed him full on the lips.

'Sleep in peace, *motaung ea motle, phomola ka khotso, Tau, phomola,* those who killed you shall know no peace. They have murdered peace, the innocent peace. The owner of the land shall rest no more. The land grabber shall sleep no more. The land capturer has murdered peace, the innocent peace. Peace that knits up worn out human relations. The ointment of stinking and bleeding relative wounds. Balm of hurt family relations. The very glue of loose marriage ties. The knot that ties siblings together. Chief nourisher of Earth stability. The spring, the head, the fountain of our life, is stopped; the very source of it is stopped. Avenged shall your death be'.

After this brave talk with her husband the mother was recharged and refreshed. She laid his head gently on the ground and covered him. The mother walked to the hip of their belongings and searched for a clean ironed spotless sheet. The tight circle of men and women kept still and silent. Only their eyes followed every move the mother made. She found the white sheet she was looking for. Ironed and spotless. The mother came back to the circle. They opened an entrance for her and closed without speaking. The mother walked with dignity and held her head high. She walked for the family and held her posture straight and tall for the family. Two women and two men helped the mother to wrap the body. Wrapping of the body was done in absolute dignity and silence.

The children of the dead man were quite and silent. They know that their father has just died but strange, they did not flinch, they did not roll on the ground in loud burst of cries, they did not cry. One sob and one drop of tear and quickly wiped off and a brave look and that was all. How strange! Children can surprise you.

Children are clever and proud and calculating. They are ashamed to cry in front of strangers and they become more accepting and mature.

I remember when I was just a little boy my mother took me every week to Tshepong Hospital for eye treatment. The other week instead of mother taking me to hospital herself, she entrusted me to a stranger—a domestic worker next door. She gave me five cents and said: "Matsime behave yourself, I know you are a good boy."

At the hospital the doctor and his assistant placed me on a big chair, they fastened my legs and my waist and my arms and my head to the chair. The doctor stood next to my head with the longest syringe I ever saw and he said: "Simon, I am going to inject your eyes. Please do not make any move, do not even move your eyelids or your eye balls. Open your eyes wide. If you try to move or scream, your eyes shall be damaged and you shall walk back home without them and you shall never see Mittah again." And so I behaved.

Many years later we had a talk about my troubling eyes and I asked: "Mama, tell me why you gave me a stranger on that day of injection."

"Why, because if I, myself, could have accompanied you on that day, you could have screamed and kicked and squawked and leaped and broken the doctors chair and lost an eye or two."

Life began to move again. This group of men and women became a unit bound together by empathy to the strangers. One woman in the group offered that the body may be temporarily taken into her enclosure from the public eyes. Her husband objected saying that that shall be an omen or doom of inviting death to their own family. The mother also objected saying that it shall be like giving away her husband's body by laying it down in another woman's bedroom and thanked the woman for her offer.

The men and women began to work. There was a self appointed woman leader in the group. She ordered this and that. Men were ordered to erect the enclosure for the new arrivals. All obliged. The mother remained sitting next to the body and ordered that the enclosure should enclose them, right around into the center.

The evening came and the women shared the little food they have with the children and the mother. Two women and two men offered to guard the body through out the night in the new enclosure. The group held night prayers and sang praises to God before dispersing. The body shall be taken to the mortuary tomorrow morning. The group assures the mother that they shall be readily available through this time of sadness. She was deeply thankful.

Later the mother said to the women: "It is odd, the passing on of my husband does not make me feel any different from what I felt before. I do not feel sadder than I was before. It is just the same thing, Tau and the land; they were just the same thing. And my husband did not die here. He died the minute he was forced off the land onto the back of a truck. He remained on the land. He could not leave it. I did not take him serious in the middle of a trip when after a long silent sleep he opened his eyes and asked me: 'Mama to where is this man taking you? To which skunk place is he taking my children?' It is only now that I realise by saying this and kissing our—" Then their last born—the father's most beloved, burst out into a loud cry and threw himself onto her mother's lap. I do not know but if the other woman was not obstructing his way maybe he could have thrown himself on top of his father's body.

In the morning of the first day it dawned to the mother and children that truthfully people can not live in a squatter camp. No right thinking man or woman will ever choose to live in a squatter camp. Summarily, although they live in a democratic South Africa, these people have no right to choose where to live. They are forced by poverty and injustice to die in the squatter camp. There are no yards to call your own. No piece of space for your children to play on. No space to erect a long drop toilet. All that is yours is four by four meters of land on which your skunk shelter stands. The toilet is a public toilet, not the public you know, but the most public—a toilet without walls. The water can not quench thirst, it is lukewarm and tastes bad and smells very bad. The water is collected from a delivery truck that has no timetable, it may come every day of the week or only once in a week. It may come early in the morning or late in the afternoon.

The water delivery truck stands towards the centre of the skunk place and then children and mothers—heavily pregnant and not, fathers and old men—drunk and half drunk all run to it. They trip and fall as they run to it because first come gets water and last gets dry. At the end of the hose pipe there is no order, they push each other and loose half of the scarcest basic resource in the skunk place. Two weeks ago a fight broke out here and a pregnant mother sustained a stab wound to the abdomen. "God of life protected both her and her child, now three days old," I am told.

"I wish God of water and God of food were as faithful as God of life, the One who never fails to give us air to breathe," a boy whose age I fail to determine adds.

The mother and children spent their first day without water because they did not know about the truck and water. Here in the skunk place you can not ask for water to drink, you must loan it. So they loaned half bucket of water to use sparingly. No bathing today and the mother begins to comprehend why people are dirty and clothed in dirt and smell dirty.

The local undertaker from the nearest town, a White man, was moved to tears this morning when he came to understand how and why the man died. He offered to do everything, storage, coffin and burial for free; out of the love of God.

"Thank you very much for your kindness, it really shows that there is still God who cares, in fact I was beginning to think that there is no God in this skunk place," the mother thanked the man.

The day of the funeral came. There was a preacher who charged the poor mother double too much to conduct the funeral. The preacher, the man of God, could not do it out of the love of God. The mother paid because her beloved husband deserved a decent funeral.

After service at home the congregation was packed into three open vans and the hearse led the way with the mother to the grave yard 37 kilometers away. "My husband will be very happy to be laid next to his father and mother; there in the grave yard of our forefathers and foremothers," the mother proudly tells the hearse driver.

They arrived back in their land but to their horror there was no grave yard and there were no graves; only a freshly cultivated piece of land. There were no standing remains of walls to prove that people ever lived on this land. The preacher standing next to the mother said: "If I am correct I would say that the arm of the Lord has struck. Or maybe is the new South Africa."

The mother was struck numb with disbelief. She thought that she was dreaming. "No, it can't be true! It must be horrible nightmare and I will awake and find that really it is different. But no I am awake and there are no graves of our past generations. "

Still numb with grief and groaning with heartache the mother cried out loud and clear: "Oh God, where are you? Oh God, do you really care? How can you let this happen to us? Are the graves of our parents also not our possession? Do they also not belong to us? The graves of our parents are gone and missing. We can not live on land and we can not die peacefully on land and we can not be buried on our graveyards next to our parents' graves on land. Our grave yard is destroyed and cultivated and turned into maize fields. Which sin surpasses the erasure of graves from the face of the earth? Graves are a physical connection that connects the living and the dead. It is a continuous relationship between the living and the dead. Death can not destroy the love of the living to the dead. Together—in life and death. To us life is such a whole that not even death can destroy. The continuity that exists between what is seen and not seen. Blessed are those who believe without seeing. To us life is an intrinsic relationship, between the Creator and creature and between the living and the dead, which death can not destroy. Today the hatred and cruelty of the owner of land has done what death can not do. How powerful is the owner of the land!" The mother fainted for the first time in her life.

The owner of the land and other owners of lands came with all kinds and models of 4x4s and dogs to drive away the people before they could dig a grave on land. People terrified and trembling quickly got back on their vehicles and drove slowly back. They must drive slowly because it is a funeral procession. The owners of lands drove the people back up to the main road. Looking back at the funeral procession of different makes of vehicles the mother smiled and said: "Surely my husband must be smiling where ever he is to see this big procession of his funeral which even includes all wealthy owners of lands in this district."

Beside the road people congregated and dug a grave and the man laid to rest. The mother said: "It is better to lay down my husband here beside the road than anywhere else because it is on this land where his people are buried." Not far from where his father is buried and beside the road the man was buried.

After the burial service the mother was exhausted and spent and looked hundred years old. She cried and climbed back on the front seat of the hearse to go back and die in the squatter camp.

After 1994, the owners of land, nervous and afraid of change have driven people out of farm lands. Nervous as horses before thunderstorm. The owners of land, nervous, fearing democracy, knowing nothing of change and democracy. The owners of land, driven by fear, mistrust of present government and hatred, the farm workers rights, labours rights, growing labour unity and government plans; not knowing these things are results, not causes. Only results, not causes.

The causes lie deep and hidden, so far so near; the causes are a hunger in the stomach, multiplied hundred times, a hunger in a single soul, and hunger for happiness and some security, multiplied thousand times; muscles and mind aching to grow, to develop, to work, and to create, multiplied million times. The very God given right and responsibility to a human being— muscles aching to work, mind aching to create beyond the single need. This is what makes a person, a real human being—*motho tota*. The whole cake of charity and grants and food parcels can not satisfy this hunger and desire. A need and desire to be whole and to be what God created him or her to be. Because a human being, unlike any other creature on planet earth, grows beyond his work, walks up the stairs of his concepts, emerges ahead of his accomplishments. Hunger for being contented can not be satisfied by the whole cake of heaven and earth but by happiness, security, development and self reliance of the individual human being.

The owners of land insensible of the suffering of multitudes; insensible because their wealth and life in abundance cut them off apart from the suffering multitudes and place them high above them, a class somewhere between heaven and earth. They are a superior class of superior wealth and luxury, totally different from the class of the poor. A class created as the results of colonisation and apartheid. This is what makes them to be indifferent and insensible and uncaring to the plight of the poor. They see themselves as creatures apart and different from the poor. The quality of owning freezes them into 'us' and cuts them off for ever from the 'people'. Instead of easing the pain and oppression of poverty it seems they derive pleasure in making the lives of the poor worse. They know that the widening gap between the haves and the have not's shall forever preserve their superior class. Apartheid or democracy theirs is a class above the rest and people dying in poverty in the squatter camps and locations and townships are not their people. They are skunks of the world; to use the words Nelson Mandela used on his inauguration in 1994.

The owners of the land are unsettled and suspicious. They are suspicious of this peace and this present government. They know that the land question, although not spoken out, is on the forefront of the people minds, especially the suffering and downtrodden. They know that these people have suffered and many of them died for the land.

One man, one family driven from the land like a skunk, on the back of a lorry to a squatter camp. In the evening a man sits outside and thinks: 'I lost my home. I lost my possessions. I am alone and I am frightened'. And in the dark of night the man tells it to the neighbour squatter. And women and children listen.

Hey! You, who fear change and block better life for all; keep these two squatting men apart; make them hate, fear and suspect each other, make them blame democracy and government. Make them blame the Councillor and the Mayor and the MEC and the Premier and the President. Lie to them that corruption is to be blamed, not colonisation and apartheid. Tell them that colonisation and apartheid died many years ago with their effects and results. Tell me how long shall your lies hold?

Keep these two squatting men apart because they are the root of what you fear. This is the zygote. For here 'I lost my home and my possessions' is changed; a cell is split and from its splitting grows the thing you hate—'We lost our homes and our possessions.' The danger is here, because two men are not as lonely and frightened as one.

And from this first 'we' there grows a still more dangerous thing: 'I have a little food', then it grows horns into 'I have no food'. If from this problem the two squatting men add up correctly and get the sum of 'We have a little food' and they add up again and get 'We have no food', then the thing is on its way, the movement has direction. Now only a little multiplication is needed to get 'I have been dispossessed of my home and my possessions on my motherland', you just add one and the sum is 'We have been dispossessed of our homes and our possessions on our motherland'. This is the thing that you must bomb and kill, the 'we' thing. Because this thing 'we' is fearless and powerful.

One day the 'we' thing shall stand up and say enough is enough, and now is the time; to march from the dumping sites back to the land and occupy the motherland. That day is coming. Like a wind is in the air. That day shall be here. And machine guns and canons and tanks and bombs and tear gas shall not stop the march of the people. We better wake up and do something now to avert that day and keep it from ever coming.

Hey! Wake up! Come up to logic and sense and reason and reality and truth. If you who own the things people must have could understand this, you shall save us all, yourself included. If you could separate causes from results, if you could know that what happened in Zimbabwe are the results, not causes, and are bound to happen in South Africa if the status quo remains. If you could know that Zimbabwe, Sudan, Burundi, Rwanda, Kenya, Uganda, Tunisia, Egypt, Yemen, Libya, Russia, and France are the results, not causes, we might survive.

THE TRUTH

Lie to me 'cause truth is pain
Truth is gold
Like gold that goes through hammering
Hammering and drilling and fire
So the truth is
It hammers and drills and fires
People inside

My Country, South Africa

Hey! Wake up! The war is raging!
It is eating up you children
it is finishing up your children
it is consuming up your children
The raging war is not of bombs and artillery
For not alone by war of arms a nation falls
The microbes of fear, hate and poverty
Like an HIV/AIDS in the blood
Eats up the fleshy tissue of the nation
Eats up your children
My country, justice cannot prevail
In the presence of victimisation and favouritism
Prosperity is annihilated by corruption
People die in extreme poverty
My country, justice cannot prevail
In the presence of continuous suffering
As the results of colonisation and apartheid

South Africa turns to God
For guidance, wisdom and fearless hearts
To push forward to *change for the good*
So that God's will happens on earth as it is in
Heaven

WAR

In a war all are not winners
In a war all are losers
Even the winner is not real
He is a loser
All are losers because all
All have lost something
Something and someone
Someone fallen
Fallen never to rise up again
Fallen where he stood
Where he stood for
For a bloody stinking war
No winners all wimping losers
All their victories add up to less
To less than what they could have gained
Without war

PEACE

How beautiful you are
Like a bride in the morn of ululations
Sweet like a heart of water lemon
Serene like a child on mother's breast
Contented like lotto winner
True peace how just, fair and noble you are!

Blessed are those who know you
Who seek and dwell in you
Who water your tree
And reside on its shade

Peace the innocent and just
How proper you are
How fair and just you must be
To knit up worn out human relations

To seal bleeding relative wounds
To balm hurt family relations
And glue loose marriage ties
The knot that ties siblings together
The chief nourishment of prosperity
The spring, the fountain, the very source of our lives

How inseparable you are
With love and justice
Peace, love and justice together
Together are strong and infinite
Peace without the two limps
Only brittles and fleeting a ways
Peace that stands endlessly
Is corner stoned and locked
On truth, love and justice

IN 2011 APARTHEID DEAD BUT STILL SUFFER

*"Apartheid is keeping apart different racial groups
by allocating separate living areas for them".*

Whenever I see RDP houses
I see black people
Wherever I see RDP houses
I see black people

Whenever I see RDP houses
I see stinking poverty
Wherever I see RDP houses
I see stinking poverty

Whenever I see big mansions
I see white people
Wherever I see big mansions
I see white people

Whenever I see big mansions
I see abundant wealth
Wherever I see big mansions
I see abundant wealth

RDP houses and black people
And poverty is one
Big mansions and white people
And wealth is one

Apartheid condemns black people
Condemns them to die in poverty
Apartheid preservers white people
Preservers them to live in abundance

Go and tell it to your chickens
Tell them that there is no apartheid
No apartheid in the new South Africa
Tell them that there is equality
Tell them that one is equal to thousand
Tell them that black people are happy
Are happy and as happy as white people
Tell them that one is equal to ten thousand
Tell them that one is equal to million
Tell them, tell them, tell them
They are your chickens
They can not think

DYING IN POVERTY

People in squatter camps are condemned to die in squatter camps because
they can not live or make a living in the squatter camp.

From nothing to nothing is not life at all. Living life is about climbing
from height to height of achievement and happiness and suffers a setback
here or there. Living life is about in spite of challenges you continue to

climb the ladder of success towards self-actualisation and deep satisfaction. Remember Maslow's hierarchy of needs.

Life is the mixture of great quantity of happiness and very small quantity of sadness.

I should remind you that dying like death is sadness. Dying is about moving from depth to depth of sadness, from depth to depth of pain and suffering. Its music is composed of a single note of sadness.

Like in dying, there is no happiness at all in the squatter camp. The food parcels and government grants are a temporary transport out of pain of sadness and suffering. It is only to take them out of their bleakness for a time.

CRY FOR MOTHERLAND

Thousand people marching
Thousand people homeless
Homeless in their homeland
Homeland with no home
Homeland with no land
Land of their birth
Land of their forefathers
Home built with their sweat
Home built with their hands
Wiped off the home land

Ten thousand people waiting
Waiting and waiting and waiting
Waiting for RDP houses
Waiting for tap water
Waiting for electricity
Waiting for tar road
Waiting for charity
Waiting for school
Waiting for grant
Waiting for clinic

Hundred thousand people marching
Marching for job creation
Marching for service delivery
Marching for salary increment
Marching against racism
Marching against victimisation
Marching against injustice
Marching and moving in circles
Every year to nowhere
Marching and begging at the same time
Public system stretched to the extreme
Private system and ownership napping
Napping on top of seventy percent
Of land and wealth of the country
And the land lay vacant and fallow
And the people are homeless and landless
Because their country and government have no land
Is like top dogs came with the land to motherland
Came with land in their pockets to our motherland
And us her children remain underdogs and landless

LAND UP FOR GRABS

The man comes flying
From across the seas
He is a European man
With a passport to visit
He touches down at O. R.
A black limousine sneaks the man
Quickly for a deal in a five star hotel
For a man from Europe is propitious
His piece of land in Johannesburg
Has got a bidding buyer
At twenty million rand

His piece of land in Johannesburg
The man has never bought it
The man has never walked on it
The man has never worked it
The man has never touched it
The man has never smelled it
Or felt it after soft rain
The man has never seen it
Except for figures on paper
The European man born in Europe
And his father born in Europe
His grandfather grabbed this piece
While on visit to South Africa in 1913
1913 Land Act was land up for grabs
For any one who happened to be White
Land up for grabs from the Blacks

Up for grabs from the rightful owners
Up for grabs to the land grabbers
And today our people still suffer
Because of this 1913 injustice
The skunks are the results of 1913
1913 is the cause and the root
1913 must be uprooted by the justice system
Or by the people who rightfully belong
To South Africa the motherland

Every child has the right to suck milk from its mother
1913 sneaked that from Black South Africans
Blacks were driven from springs, rivers, hills and valleys
And still settle in semi dry places and suffer poverty

Every child has a right to play on the lap of its mother
1913 stole that from Black South Africans
Blacks were driven as skunks from the land
Today are settled in squatter camps next to dumping
places and sewerages

Every child has the right to enjoy the love and wealth of its mother
Unjust laws grabbed that from Black South Africans
Still today they work very hard digging platinum,
diamond and gold
Not for South Africa but for AngloGold

SQUATTER CAMP

The place of need and lack
The place of defeat and loss
The place of sadness and worry
The place of cry and discomfort
The place of the worse of worst
The place of cold and winter floods
The place of hunger and foodlessness
The place of thirst and burning hot shelters
The place of utmost indecency and worst life
The place of no remainders but severity and extremes
The place of people reduced to the skunks of the world
The place of waiting and waiting and waiting

Families huddled together
Clustered and bunched as skunks
Families bundled together
Bundled on top of each other
Bundled and tight firm
Bundled tight and painful
With poverty bundle strap
Caught in the strap that is perpetual
With no room or chance to escape from/to
(In) the land of beauty and plenty and abundance
Forced to live die in the world of horror and need

Squatter camp the school that dehumanises children
Teaches them to be a lesser people
Robs them of hope and love
And become the don't cares
And the nothings to lose
In the world and of the world
Hate life and rejoice in death
The heartless criminals of our day
That robs South Africa of safety and security

Peace and poverty is dove and wolf
People do not live in squatter camps
People only die in squatter camps
A slow long-drawn-out painful d—e—a—t—h

LOVE

Once in elementary school
To prevent others teasing her lack
A little girl picks up a little stone
Without her little friends seeing
Puts it in her mouth
And sucks it like a sweets
As orphans do
As poor do

Realising the little girl
Another little girl
Laughs not—others do
Jokes not—others do
Teases not—others do
Takes out her packet of sweets
And shares with her

She remains with sweets
She gains love
She gains true friend

She lost nothing
Others lost a friend
And gained a shame

This illustrates that we are born with love.
Loving and sharing are intrinsic in human
beings. You need not go to school or
university to love your neighbour—your
fellow human being.

RDP

RDP is not Revenge of the Dark People
RDP is less Reconstruction and Development Programme
I see RDP houses I see loss
I see RDP houses I see suffering
I see RDP houses I see hunger
I see RDP houses I see death
I see RDP houses I see poverty
I see RDP houses I see black people
Why mainly black people
They were relegated by apartheid
To die in poverty
RDP is more Relegation to Die in Poverty
RDP is nothing but a badge of poverty
A black man is forced to beg for it and die in it
A condition of deepest humiliation and absolute dependency
Results perpetrated by apartheid and its policies
A condition of helplessness, hopelessness
Powerlessness, homelessness, landlessness
Moneylessness, foodlessness and lifelessness
RDP is nothing but Relegation to Die in Poverty
RDP is nothing but BBP—Badge of Black Poverty

THE TRC OF 1994

Peace and reconciliation were very fundamental and necessary and relevant for the establishment of the new democratic government of the Republic of South Africa.

Peace was very enticing especially to the Blacks who were hungry for peace after suffering for a long time as a result of being the major focus of slaughtering and victims of war against apartheid.

After the bombs and machine guns and war tanks and tear gas and slaughtering and all kinds of ammunition and atrocities stopped, the Black people emerged battered and wounded and bleeding and limping from exile and imprisonment and dispossession and massive agony. They were tired and exhausted by war and their aim was to achieve peace in their lifetime; at all costs.

The Truth and Reconciliation Commission (TRC) was established. I think the TRC became the biggest injustice show on stage and off-stage of the new South Africa. Most white apartheid leaders who were in parliament and other spheres of government refused to cooperate with the TRC.

"What could we do to the all mighty and powerful?" one man asked, and said: "They escaped scot free and preserved their white supremacy and white privilege."

Once I gave five year olds, each of them, a packet of sweets and banana. They continued enjoying their games as if they did not notice my gifts and I went back to my study room.

A while later I heard a bitter cry from one of them. I looked out through the window and realised that his banana and sweets were stolen. He was angry and sad and refused to play.

The other one felt sorry for him; she approached him and said: "I have taken away your banana and sweets. It was my fault and I regret it. I will never do it again."

She ran and disappeared under the big tree and came with his packet of sweets and banana.

"Please forgive me and here take your packet of banana and sweets," she pleads.

With a big smile the boy stretched out his hands to accept the giving back of his packet.

With a soft voice the girl asked: "Would you then play with us?"

The boy answered with a beautiful smile: "Yes, because I have received all that is mine and I have forgiven you."

True peace and true reconciliation require **the truth**, **regret**, **sincere apology**, **giving back** or **equivalent payback**, **acceptance** and **forgiveness**. These six ingredients of what we still need to do in South Africa, I learnt them not at the university but from five year olds playing in my backyard.

The first four ingredients in the well cooked TRC pot must be the roles and responsibilities willingly performed by the perpetrators. The last two are the responsibilities of recovered and pleased victims. And thus true peace and true reconciliation and true unity shall grow and develop naturally. In a true TRC people must be given a platform to bring Sol Plaatje's words of 'all we claim is our just dues' into reality.

F.W. de Klerk made insincere apology that apartheid was vicious, but its perpetrators were innocent because they were not vicious; he made an example of his father that he had helped to implement apartheid and his father was not a vicious man. The whole former head of state and head of apartheid government reasoned like, I think, a naughty little boy who throws stones and put blame on stones for breaking windowpanes.

A delegation of Mfengu leaders met De Klerk to plead for the return of their land from which they had been forcibly removed. One leader pleaded with him: "I used to have land, I used to have cattle, I used to have sheep, and I used to have my own house. I am seventy years of age. Now I have nothing." And this cry elicited not even a token gesture of regret from de Klerk or his gang or *sy ooms*.

De Klerk continued to refuse to take the blame or responsibility of the misery suffered by the Black people: "It was not our intention to deprive people of their rights and to cause misery (it was apartheid), but eventually apartheid led to just that."

The racists Whites did very little or nothing to bring about true peace and true reconciliation and they walked away with everything except the presidential seat of the Republic of South Africa.

P.W. Botha, the former apartheid leader, was also supposed to take responsibility and make apology for the atrocities and miseries caused during his tenure as the former head of apartheid government. Instead of Botha being subpoenaed by the TRC to appear before it in Cape Town, Desmond Tutu went to see him in his daughter's home in George.

Tutu and Botha had a balanced two-hour discussion over tea and melktert. Botha denied any wrong or evil on his part and therefore made no apologies.

About appearing in front of the TRC he palpably refused, totally without remainder.

Unconventional option is offered.

President P.W.Botha agrees to provide written answers to questions from the TRC.

TRC questions are delivered to Botha.

Months passed while the TRC was waiting for Botha's answers.

P.W. Botha unilaterally breaks the agreement.

The TRC makes a very brave decision—subpoena him.

The date came and Botha did not come to the TRC.

Later Botha said he could not attend because of illness.

The TRC scheduled a new date.

TRC was prepared to hold hearings in his home town, George, he refused.

President Nelson Mandela offered to accompany Botha to the TRC, he refused.

The date came and passed by and there was no Botha.

This time Botha said: "I don't appear in circuses."

The case of Botha and the TRC went on.

In its main report, issued in 1998, the TRC identified Botha as "the man who took the State into the realms of criminality."

But I doubt if Botha ever bothered to get a copy of that report.

And so what do you think about the TRC?

In 1990 Desmond Tutu thought that if South Africans were to overcome the damage apartheid had caused they have to face up to its results one by one and work through them. For this reconciliation to happen, he said, those responsible for apartheid first had to confess their sin: "We have wronged you and hurt you by this apartheid and its injustices, by uprooting you from your lands and homes, by dumping you in poverty-stricken homeland resettlement camps, by giving your children inferior education, and 'denying that you are human beings' by denying you human rights. We are sorry; forgive us." Tutu further said that those who had committed wrongs had to make restitution: "If I have stolen your pen, I can't really be contrite when I say, 'Please forgive me,' if at the same time I still keep your pen. If I am truly repentant, I will demonstrate this genuine repentance by returning your pen."

I think that the great father of the people, Desmond Tutu, was somehow forced to preside over something totally different from what he initially thought and desired.

Because the Black people came to the TRC wounded, limping, battered, bleeding and hopeful but they went back to poverty-stricken resettlement camps and squatter camps and new smaller shelters known as RDP houses wounded, limping, battered, bleeding, not as bad as they came but worse because they sadly left without hope but poverty stricken more than before.

THE TRC

Truth and Reconciliation Commission
No, it was less that
I think TRC was more
Tasked and Responsible to Conceal apartheid
Apartheid and its beneficiaries
Tasked to protect its beneficiaries
To forgive and forget apartheid
Apartheid and its beneficiaries
Its beneficiaries continue to benefit
To benefit and live life
Life of white supremacy and wealth
Its victims continue to suffer
To suffer and die in poverty
Its victims suffered in the old South Africa
Its victims suffer in the new South Africa
Suffering and suffering and suffering
And hope shrinks and shrinks and shrinks

The old South Africa

It was a place of two tales
It was a place of sadness and happiness
It was a place of lack and abundance

It was a place of black and white
It was a place of death and life
It was a place of living life
It was a place of dying life
It was horrible it was beautiful
It was a place of white is right
It was a place of black is wrong
It was right it was wrong
It was fair is foul and foul is fair
It was right is wrong and wrong is right
It was serene and hurly-burly at the same time

It was a place where a black child inherited nothing
Nothing but a life long curse of being born black
A black child born into poverty and die in poverty
It was a place where a white child inherited wealth
And nothing but wealth and nice life
White man enjoying the extraordinary wealth and ease
It was a place where a black man was not allowed to live
But die in poverty
It was a place where a white man was enabled to live
And celebrate life on daily basis

A NATION OF BEGGARS

A nation of beggars in the making
A nation born without a choice to live
But die every day slowly into begging
A nation born without a choice to work
Without a choice to earn a living
Without a choice to lead a decent life
But condemned to life of indecency
Living from hand to mouth
A life of waiting and waiting and waiting

The month end comes a little grant comes
The mother is faced with extremely

Difficult decision making
It is winter—buy a jersey for the school?
Or buy a pair of school shoes?
What about the food debt at the shop?
Monthly contributions to church?
What if the funeral policy laps again?
I am sick and going from this hardship
But what about my dear twins?
Can not pay the church or the undertaker?
But I will love to have both for my funeral

Oh I forgot about the school trip
The school trip I promised them to pay
To pay this month when the grant comes
The grant has come and there is no money for the trip
This poverty changes people to become liars
Liars In the eyes of their little children
This poverty makes people to become
To become that which they are not
Liars and skunks and alcoholics and little thieves
Little thieves that graduate to become hardened criminals
Hardened and hart lessened criminals
That all South Africa suffers from

This new South Africa

This new South Africa
It is not what the people died for
This new South Africa falls far short
Far shot of Black people's expectations
It is not what the Black people suffered for
This new South Africa is not worth their loss
It is not worth the loss of Black people
This new South Africa has detained Blacks
Detained them in a state of permanent transition
Transition and permanent death in poverty and agony

Ensures perpetual White economic dominance and opulence
The new South Africa is nothing but the old wine in a new bottle

The Black man toiling and sweating
In the garden in a hot summer day
Laboring exhaustedly expecting a pay
A pay of one hundred rand at the end of the day
Only to be forced to accept a pay
A pay of ten rand at the end of the day
The poor Black man is also forced
Also forced not to grumble
The Black man is forced to bend
The Black man shall break or burst
The Black man shall break or burst
The Black man shall break or burst

Andries Tatane of Ficksburg

The Black man breaking and bursting
Breaking and bursting
Breaking and bursting the chains
The unbroken chains
The unbroken chains of colonisation
The unbroken chains of apartheid
The unbroken chains of enslaved life
The unbroken chains of poverty

Tatane suffered *en genoeg* of suffering
Pierced by the thorns of lack
Punctured by the horns of lack
Pinched by the dashes of death
Death of the dead living in poverty

Tatane breaking and bursting
Bare handed and bare half bodied
Defenseless and unarmed
Challenges the cannon and the armed
Tatane is summarized by the armed
Down and beaten Tatane is shot and killed

Killed by the armed of colonised minds
Killed by the armed of apartheited minds
Killed by the armed chained by the unbroken chains
Unbroken chains Tatane fought to free them from

DEDICATION TO MY MOTHER
—MAMA MMITAH

She was, a mother she was
A true mother
Loving and caring none stop

She was, a mother she was
A proper mother
Her love to me
Existed up to the end of her existence
And I believe it still exists beyond

She was, a mother she was
A sweet mother
She was a precious jewel of my life
She illuminated every breath I took
Through out my very existence
Upon this hour and the shawl of time
She was always by my side
Her love had no limits
Her support had no boundaries
She could see things which I could never see
And she saw them clearly
She could say things and then I took them simply
Only now I realise how fundamental her sayings were
And now I wish she was here so that we could talk all over again
Nna ga ke a tsalwa ke mosadi—Ke tsetswe ke Mosadisadi!
Hela banna! Nna ga ke a tsalwa ke mosadi
Ke tsetswe ke mosadi wa basadi
Mosadi tota—Mosadisadi
A Mosadi!

DEDICATION TO MY FATHER —DANIEL KGASA MOHAPI

Hela banna! Utlwang ke a boka
Nna ha ke boke ke ba a mabala
Ke ba a mabala a nkwe ke tshwaa mabaka

Lebang Kgasa ka matlhong o maribitla
Ha a maribitla ke matlho a Tau
Ke Tau, ke Motaung
Ke motho o borra Thulo-Mphete
Ke motho o borra Mosunye
Tebetebe ya Moletsane
Makitlane motho oa sebelebele
Motho oa ho tsalwa ke Makoeje le Mosunye
Mohapi-Mohapi ka sebele! Mohapi ha bedi
Monna oa ho katoha monyo
Ho bona se tladi e sejang
Ke motho ea e reng a hata a hatoha
Seadimo nkgono a re: Ya tlang ke Kgasa, ke Makitlane
Ba re: O mo bona jang o sa bone?
A re: Ke utlwa ka lefatshe ho thothomela

Helehelele! Bomme le bontate
Hloang tsebe ke roneketse Motaung
Hei! Rona re tsetswe ke Mosadisadi
Tlase'a maoto a monna oa Motaung
A potipotiloe ke makanyane ka hohlehohle
Nyamatsana di lapetse ho re metsa
Ntata'a rona Tau, Kgasa, Makitlane
A e loana e mahlo mafubedu
A duma a paruma ha a bona makanyane
Makanyane a batla ho re metsa
A duma a paruma, dipoa le tsona tsa paruma
E le fa dithota le tsona di a rabela
Makanyane a nyelela ka ponyo ya leitlho
A sia a sa leba kwa morago
Ha ba ha utlwala bo peperr-perr—peperr-perr
E le fa mala a dira a berekega

Fa e duma tlase lefatsheng Tau
Dipoa le dithota di a rabela
Lentswe la ba la tlhaha lehodimong
La re: Ho duma eng tlase lefatsheng?
Ba araba ba re: Ke Tau; ke Sebata
Ke Tshehla, e feditse!
A e hate ka maro'
Makwala a none!

www.ingramcontent.com/pod-product-compliance
Lightning Source LLC
Chambersburg PA
CBHW020259290526
45784CB00003B/1301